THE ETHIOPIAN SERVANT OF CHRIST:

The Life of Father Abd el-Mesih el-Habashi

The
Ethiopian
Servant of Christ

The Life of Father Abd el-Mesih el-Habashi

---

by His Grace Bishop Macarius

ST SHENOUDA'S MONASTERY PRESS
SYDNEY, AUSTRALIA
2009

THE ETHIOPIAN SERVANT OF CHRIST:

The Life of Father Abd el-Mesih el-Habashi

COPYRIGHT © 2009
ST. SHENOUDA COPTIC ORTHODOX MONASTERY

First published in Arabic by El Baramouse Monastery, 1996.
Translated to English by Michael Kosman.

St Shenouda Coptic Orthodox Monastery
8419 Putty Rd,
Putty, NSW 2330
Sydney, Australia

www.stshenoudamonastery.org.au

ISBN 13: 978-0-9805171-3-2

Cover Design:
Peter Botros,
Bot Dezign Pty Ltd
www.botdezign.com.au

Contents

ABOUT THE AUTHUR

His Grace Bishop Macarius, is an
Auxiliary Bishop for the Holy Metropolis of
El Minya, and Abou Qurqas, Assistant to
His Eminence Metrapolitan Arsenius.

FOREWARD

*"The Great Man from the Cave...
Departed to Jerusalem"*

MONASTICISM OF THIS CHRISTIAN ERA has not known a monk who lived the life of continuous solitude to the degree of Father Abd el-Mesih el-Habashi. He lived all the facets of the ascetic life fully, bearing the famous name Father Abd el-Mesih el-Habashi (the Ethiopian).

He was born into a very wealthy family in Ethiopia, and he received education from one of its schools. When he realised that his teachers took special interest in him due to his intelligence, he decided to leave the world and go to the monastery. When he could not accommodate to the life in the monastery, he departed from there and went to live in the Shehete desert. He came to it from Ethiopia on foot, and he joined the Baramous Monastery. He then left the monastery and lived in a cave alone. He faced many great hardships in the beginning, but he stood strong until he settled in.

Father Abd el-Mesih el-Habashi spent more than forty-five years fasting, never once eating meat, fish, or any dairy products. At some periods in his life, the only thing he ate was breadcrumbs. He stayed in his cell for many decades. I myself was a disciple of his for a period of my monastic life.

Anybody who visited him said that he told them to sit down with him on the ground, and he would talk to them about the Bible. He was very strict about the truth, and following the Lord's commandments and the rules of monasticism. One of the people who took care of the needs of Father Abd el-Mesih el-Habashi, and supplied him with food and clothes, was Bishop Theophilus the abbot of the Surian Monastery.

His asceticism is inspirational...

Finally, Father Abd el-Mesih el-Habashi dearly wished that he could spend his last days in Jerusalem, so he came to Cairo and insisted that I approve his departure to Jerusalem on foot! After long discussions, he finally agreed on taking a ship to Syria and from there to Jerusalem.

by H.H. Pope Shenouda III

PREFACE

FR ABD EL-MESIH EL-HABASHI is one man who was not concerned about anything or for anyone. His only concern was for the One; his eyes were directed towards eternity. He was content with enough food sufficient to keep him alive and enough clothing to cover his nakedness. He chose God as his way as well as his means.

He unintentionally attracted us to him through sharing and exchanging the many tales that thousands of people have experienced in mixed feelings of wonder, joy, and deep contemplation. The multitude of people who saw him and dealt with him have all attested to that lion who carries the heart of a child. He had a clear vision and a way of life. He did not act haphazardly but his behavior was a result of deep spiritual understanding.

Fr Abd el-Mesih's character combines the weakness of the human nature and the strength of the spiritual personality. He was not of a special breed of people, like anyone he was agitated, tasted pain, and suffered trials. He left all these experiences for us as an example in persevering in trials. He lived an austere ascetic life and experienced many hardships. The devil waged many wars against him but he escaped them all.

The best portrayal of this saint's life is the following few lines that were said of St Pisarioun in the Paradise of Pelladius:

"It was said about abba Pisarioun that he was like the birds of heaven, and like one of the beasts of the wilderness. He completed his life in solitude without worry. He did not care to have a dwelling place or to store food. He never owned a book or clothing. His life was free of all bodily passions holding fast to his faith in God; he sojourned in this world by faith of things to come, wondering in the desert like a stranger, enduring all trials joyfully."

When I started collecting information about this father, I heard and read numerous stories from firsthand accounts or those who heard of him. I did not give much attention to miracles as I did to the way of life and thought of this man. I will try to concentrate on his way of life without ignoring his miracles.

All the information in this book are documented in either voice recordings or written accounts of Metropolitans, Bishops, Priests, Monks, or Lay people, who gratefully supplied me with stories and photos that they had for this great father.

May the Lord make the life of this Holy Father a source of blessing to all who read it. With the prayers of our beloved father Pope abba Shenouda III and his partner in the apostolic ministry Bishop Isodoros the Bishop and abbot of the Baramouse Monastery.

by H.G. Bishop Macarius

INTRODUCTION

CHRISTIANITY STARTED IN ETHIOPIA in the time of the Apostles, when a eunuch of great authority under Candace queen of the Ethiopians was baptised by the hands of St Phillip (Act 8:26-40). After his return to Ethiopia he told the Queen of his encounter, so she declared Christianity to be the official religion of Ethiopia. The king who succeeded Queen Candace forced Christian to put on a blue ribbon on their shoulders to distinguish them from the pagans. The Christians did so happily but they sawed crosses on this ribbon which they called (matb).

During the papacy of Saint Athanasius (365-297) AD, a rich merchant and his two sons Frumentius and Aedesius, were shipwrecked at one of the neighboring ports to Ethiopia, where they killed the father and the servants who came with him, and spared the lives of Frumentius and Aedesius. When the king of Ethiopia saw the boys he loved them and gave them a job in his palace. After the kings death the two brothers wanted to go back to their homeland but the queen asked them to stay with her until one of her sons is enthroned.

After the new king was enthroned the two brothers went to their homeland. Later on Frumentius went to Alexandria to express to St Athanasius the need of the Ethiopian people for a shepherd to look after the church and the spiritual needs of the congregation. St Athanasius seeing the zeal of Frumentius, decided to ordain him a bishop over all of Ethiopia in the year 330 AD by the name Salama (Father of Peace) or Kesate Berhan (Revealer of light)..

From this we see the close links from the beginning between the Ethiopian and Coptic Church. The tradition begun by St Athanasius continued until the late 50s of the 20th century with the Patriarch of Alexandria sending the 'Abuna' to lead the Ethiopian Church.

The Ethiopian Monastic Tradition

The fifth century saw an important development with the arrival of a group of monks from Egypt. They established monasteries which became very important centers of learning and evangelization. It would indeed be true to say that all evangelization and all education in Christian Ethiopia was in the hands of monks until modern times. Many of these monasteries are still flourishing e.g. that of Debre Damo near the Eritrean border, still only accessible by rope.

These monks translated the Bible into Ge'ez probably using the Septuagint for the Old Testament. They also translated some extra books as well as monastic writings so that the Ethiopian canon is much more extensive than any other church.

So there has been a continuous monastic tradition in Ethiopia from this time though there are some gaps in our historical knowledge. Further declined in the 9th century and later the Zagwe dynasty emerged which was responsible in the 12th century for the famous churches at Lalibella carved out of the solid rock and recognized as one of the architectural wonders of the world.

The great monastic revival of the 14th century led to the establishment of the monastery now known as Debre Libanos whose founders were St Tekle Haimanot and St Ewstatewos two very great influential Christian leaders through whom the monks of today trace their origins. The number of monks and nuns before 1908 has reached 12000, in 800 monasteries

In their extremes of austerity the monks provide a prophetic and eschatological ministry in the Ethiopia Church. The bahtawi are an independent class of hermits who represent the anchoritic tradition – modern successors of St John the Baptist rebuking all including the emperor himself without fear or favour. Some live completely separately from society, unseen by all, their bones occasionally discovered after their deaths in the remotest of places. Others lived in trees (dendrites) or small holes in the ground. Often they live on leaves and bitter roots and reduce sleep to an absolute minimum. Those living in wilderness zones on the edge of the empire had the effect of expanding the empire because they invariably attracted followers. Evangelization was not systematic but the effect was to extend the frontiers of Christianity by being so successful in converting the surrounding population.

It would not be an exaggeration to say that the

spirituality of the laity in Ethiopia is essentially a monastic spirituality. Some emperors even saw themselves as monk kings. 'When Lalibella established the throne he submitted himself to a fast more severe than that of the monks because to him the kingship appeared as the monastic life'. This may have been the ideal but of course there was always a tension between this and the reality.

ONE

THE EARLY YEARS

G EBRA SADEK ISTATIUS WAS BORN in 1898 in Liban, a small village in the city of Massowa, near the Port of Asmara. Port Asmara is now the Directorate of Hemasin, part of Ethiopia.

Gebra was the eldest of six children - three boys and three girls. We know that one of his brothers' name is Rafael and that the names of two of his sisters were Lemlem (oldest) and Zhudi (youngest).

Gebra's father, Nasegih Behel, was the very rich

owner of two hundred and fifty cows. Behel was a member of a wealthy family called Bahir Dek Behel; they were related to the local mayor. His nephews are now living in Asmara, while all of his brothers moved. The first written account of him stated that he had five uncles. One uncle, Solomon, was well known, however had no children.

The boy Gebra Sadek Istatius was a shepherd. This involved his being out with the cattle every day and returning home at sunset. His parents were surprised by Gebra's actions when he kissed their knees before and after work each day.

He was taught the Bible in the towns of Duello and Jugam. In his free time, he gave explanations about the Holy Bible at St Takla's Church, his parish church in Liban.

In remembering this period, Father Abd el-Mesih says about himself, "Material things were very abundant, but the people did not to know God," and his common expression was "No Khristos" (i.e. No Christ).

Thus, Gebra sought God from the time of his youth, but could not find Him amid the deceptive traps of the world. He therefore escaped the world and went into hiding in order to find solitude. His mother did not know where he was and was grieving, until a person who came from Egypt to Ethiopia told her that her son was alive and was in Wadi el-Natroun. These events took place a little while before her departure, however his father passed away without knowing what had happened to his son.

The Start of His Monastic Life

The young Gebra Sadek went to a monastery in Ethiopia

called Sinai Monastery, perhaps in his early twenties, where he was called 'Gabra Khristos' (Servant of Christ). He lived an ascetic life in the monastery along with about five hundred other monks. They were fed only one meal a day of cooked dry bananas.[1]

An Ethiopian monk's day would start at eleven at night, when Tasbeha (midnight praises) would start. Tasbeha would continue until five in the morning, followed by the Holy Liturgy on Sundays and on saints' feast days only. After this, each monk would go to his individual cell to continue his monastic spiritual practice. Afterwards, each monk would work from eight in the morning until one in the afternoon, after which time he would go back to his cell to rest for a while until three in the afternoon, in time for his only daily meal. The monk would then spend the rest of his day in manual labour and prayers.

A large proportion of the monastery monks lived in caves scattered around the monastery. These caves were basically cavities in the rocks. The Blessed Gebra Khristos lived in these caves for some years, but neither his life in the monastic community nor his years of solitude fulfilled his heart's desire, as he saw monasticism in Ethiopia and Sudan as unauthentic.

His Language

Ethiopia has several languages. The official language is the Amharic language, but other languages such as Tigrinya (Tejrai language) also called (el-takreniah) are also used - and that was the language spoken by Father Abd el-Mesih, in addition to the Aomenian, afarina and Bilanban. However the language generally used for liturgical prayer is the Ge'ez language.

Since monasticism in Egypt was the focus of

attention of all those seeking asceticism and seclusion throughout the world, Egyptian monasteries attracted thousands of monks from all parts of the world throughout history. The Ethiopian monks, in particular, have intensified their pilgrimages to the monasteries of Egypt since late last century. The number of Ethiopian monks in the Baramous Monastery at that time, for example, was about twenty monks. Thus, Father Abd el-Mesih was determined to move north to Egypt, to the Baramous Monastery.

From Ethiopia to the Baramous Monastery

> *They wandered about in sheepskins and goatskins, being destitute, afflicted, tormented... of whom the world was not worthy. They wandered in deserts and mountains, in dens and caves of the earth (Heb 11:37-38) because of their great love for Christ the King.*
>
> - FRACTION OF THE GREAT LENT

Father Gebra Kristos departed his country after the Nativity Liturgy on the 7th January 1934, or, according to the Coptic Calendar, the 29th day of the blessed month of Kiahk in the year 1650 of the Martyrs (AM). He departed with the same motive that had made him renounce all the wealth of his father's house, leave the communal life to live in solitude, then journey towards the ascetic life in the caves of the Baramous Monastery. His decision to direct his steps to Egypt resembles a renewal of his monastic vows.

It is important to note that a person would not be able to do any of this without renouncing all of his will and personal pleasures, in other words, giving up all of his possessions and not being tied to anything or anyone, but taking refuge and having total faith in

God, who is the Good Shepherd of our souls.

Furthermore, for him to choose to travel this narrow path on foot comprises two significant points:

(1) He is a man of brave heart, since he did not care about the harm that could pursue him as a result of such a decision. His strength, nevertheless, was always fulfilled in Christ, to whom he had offered himself.

(2) During his journey from Ethiopia to Egypt, he kept his monastic rule of asceticism and prayers, as the monastic life is not limited only to life in the monastery.

He travelled about 2,500 kilometres in approximately three months. Merchants running camel convoys accompanied him for some time during his journey. At other times he was all alone in the frightening mountains and valleys, surrounded by many dangers. The most logical guess is that he walked adjacent to the Nile River, as it is one of the shortest routes to Cairo. No doubt he had put in his heart that he would suffer for the sake of Christ...hence he did not worry about difficulties.

He had strong faith: even when he lived in his cell which looked like a cave for wild animals, he refused to make a door for it. When both Father Antonios el-Suriany (H.H. Pope Shenouda III) and the departed Anba Theofilos, Abbot of the Surian Monastery, offered to make him a door, he would simply refuse and say, "Does a wolf make a door for his own den?"

When Father Gebra Kristos arrived to Sudan, he went to the Coptic Orthodox Diocese there, where he met the departed Rev Father Youhanna Salama, the secretary of the Diocese of Sudan in Khartoum. He was welcomed warmly and was given some money for his trip to Cairo.

He was praised by Christians on his way to Egypt, and they would invite him to their homes, whether in Sudan or in Upper Egypt, and according to Father Gebra Kristos, the Christians welcomed him in their "cells!"

He finally crossed the border between Sudan and Egypt. When Fr Armeya el-Baramousy asked him how he had crossed the border between Ethiopia and Sudan, and then the border between Sudan and Egypt, he answered and said that when he approached the border, he would put his staff on his shoulders, pretending to be a shepherd, and God would grant him grace in the eyes of the border guards, so they let him pass.

After about six months travelling north through Egypt, he finally reached the Cathedral in Azbakeya, where he was directed to His Holiness the late Pope Youannes the Nineteenth by fellow sons of the Pope. His Holiness asked him if he was a monk. He did not look like a monk, so he replied saying, "No" (out of humility). The pope apologetically told him that they did not accept anyone in their monasteries unless they were actually monks. He objected gently, "If I want to become a monk, wouldn't I be better off in one of the monasteries?" So the Pope smiled and patted him and allowed him to go to the monastery of his choice, which was the Baramous Monastery.

When Father Gebra Kristos enquired about the way to the monastery, the Pope advised him to go to the village of Kafr Dawood in the Behera Province, and to travel to the monastery from there.

The Coptic Musician Ragheb Moftah – who took the blessing of tending Father Abd el-Mesih el-Habashi at his house for three months – says that he used to hide the fact that he was ordained a priest out of humility. Rev Father Mansour el-Baramousy would tell the same story; he also knew about it despite Father Gebra's attempt to keep it a secret.

Also in Egypt, most probably, he met another Ethiopian monk named Rafael, who accompanied him on his trip from the Cathedral to the Baramous Monastery. No one had accompanied Father Gebra throughout his journey from Ethiopia, but it was said that Father Rafael was present with Father Gebra upon his arrival at the monastery. However, Father Rafael left the monastery only a few days after his arrival, as he was headed for St Samuel's Monastery on the Saturday of Light, that is, a week after their arrival at the Baramous Monastery.

When Father Gebra Kristos arrived at the village of Kafr Dawood, he was led to the town residence belonging to St Bishoy's Monastery, where he told the monks of his intention to travel to the Baramous Monastery. They told him to go to the village of El Khatatbah down south, then to go to the Baramous Monastery. Although this route was a longer distance, at least he could follow the dirt road. However, he did not take their advice. Wanting to take the quickest route, he decided to travel directly to the Baramous Monastery in a straight line.

Even though the path was straight, it was arid. When the pain became overwhelming, he rested. In the distance, he saw a faint light, so he walked towards it, and found that he had reached the district of Wadi el-Natroun (where the Baramous Monastery is located) so he rested there. In the morning someone led him to the monastery.

The monks from the Baramous Monastery stood

inside the gate while the bell was ringing, and after taking permission from the abbot of the monastery[2], they prepared to open the gate. Who would we expect to be knocking!

They saw a person of 1.6 metres in height, dark skinned, brown eyed, with a serious facial expression, his beard thick under his chin, and hairless cheeks. His veins stood out from under the skin on his hands and face and a cheap white cloth was tied around his head. He wore a black tunic and a tasselled scarf around his neck and was most probably barefooted!

They would also have noticed his frantic hand gestures, which he had to use to explain his wish to become a monk in the monastery, and the purpose that drove him to come all the way from Ethiopia to Wadi el-Natroun.

He should have carried with him a letter of recommendation from His Holiness the Pope for the monastery to accept him, however he did not have that letter with him. They still accepted him and his companion Father Rafael out of pity for his exhausted figure. They could not leave him outside the monastery due to the harshness of the wilderness.

His arrival and acceptance to the monastery took place on the last Friday before Good Friday of the year 1934. From that hour onward, Gebra Kristos name became Abd el-Mesih el-Habashi (the Ethiopian Servant of Christ), which is the Arabic translation of his name. He therefore became known as Abd el-Mesih el-Habashi from that time.

The Beginning of His Life in the Monastery

When the abbot of the monastery took him to his new cell, he refused it, asking instead for another cell that was not fit for anyone to live in. So insistent was he that the Abbot agreed, even though the room he chose was only about 1.5 square metres, and is located under the steps leading up to the nearby eastern tower (one of the two towers of the monastery). The cell door was made of dented tin, and the cell was humid, dark and poorly ventilated. It would not have been possible for him to sleep in it fully stretched in either direction. What is amazing is that right next to this cell was another simple cell like it, however as it was wide enough for him, he totally rejected it.

It was essential for all monks to have a job to do, because it is said that "a monk that works is tempted by one devil, but the one who does not, is tempted by a multitude of devils." The elder monks had inherited this canon from older monks, as it was mentioned in *The Paradise of the Holy Fathers* that all monks and even the Abbot of the monastery should have some sort of manual labour to keep them occupied.

The first job that was given to him by Rev Father Basillius, the Abbot of the Monastery, was to serve in the kitchen. He consistently failed – for example, he could not turn on the kerosene oven.

He also told His Grace Bishop Isaac that he was once instructed by the Abbot to make tea for some visitors. After waiting a long time the Abbot went to check on him, only to find him looking down with great confusion at the kerosene oven, which was broken on the floor. From that time, he was excused from working in the kitchen.

However some of the old monks in the Monastery claim that he used to fail on purpose so he could be given a harder job of a lower status. Bishop Isaac also agrees, since Father Abd el-Mesih el-Habashi told him, "I left the kitchen that day and laughed a lot!"

Father Youssef el-Mahreky, who used to work in the monastery kitchen at that time, said that Father Abd el-Mesih would work with enthusiasm and energy in the kitchen, and would meticulously clean all the utensils and plates without even a hint of complaint.

The other job that Father Abd el-Mesih was given, which he accepted with great joy, was sweeping the alleys and corridors of the monastery, and carrying rubbish bags outside. For about two years, he always did these jobs, and was known by all the monks to walk around the monastery with the broom always in his hand, never speaking a word to anybody.

Father Youssef also comments about this, saying, "He would start to clean the alleys and pathways in the early morning, earnestly, quietly and with a joyful smile. At night he would also come to me to learn the names of the Psalms in the Arabic language, because he used to distribute the Psalms during prayer times in the church."

And so Father Abd el-Mesih continued to work in the monastery until an incident occurred on Lazarus' Saturday in 1936 which forced some of the monks to leave.

His Journey to Solitude

At the time mentioned above, the number of monks living a life of solitude in their private cells inside the monastery far outnumbered the monks who lived in solitude outside the monastery.

Among those who lived the solitary life in a cave outside the monastery was Fr. Mina of the Baramous (the late Pope Kyrollos the Sixth).[3]

Having previously lived a life of solitude in a cave in his homeland before his arrival in Egypt, Father Abd el-Mesih considered it essential to continue the way of life that he began when he came to the monastery.

So after Fr Mina of the Baramous left his cave in support of the excluded monks, he seized his opportunity. He went and asked the Rev Father Basillius, the Abbot of the monastery, to allow him to leave and to enter the life of solitude. Contrary to what he had expected, the Abbot totally refused his proposal, and did not even allow further discussion about the matter. His refusal was the source of ongoing friction between Father Abd el-Mesih and the Abbot for some time.

The Abbot had his concerns about Father Abd el-Mesih's safety, as the life of solitude in the desert is dangerous, and the desert beasts were of a large number during that time. Despite this fact, the major problem was that he was a foreigner; he was not taken into the monastery in accordance to a written permission from the Pope, but rather for his own safety, for protection from danger outside the walls of the monastery. It did not fit the tradition of the monastery to allow one of its foreign monks to leave the monastery to live alone.

However, Father Abd el-Mesih was not at all convinced, and pressed on in his pleas. He was faced with refusal at every turn, to the extent that the Abbot gave orders that no-one should allow Father Abd el-Mesih to leave the monastery premises.

Father Abd el-Mesih el-Habashi was then directed in miraculous ways to plan his escape. He would wait until very late at night, and would climb up a palm tree, grab a few of its leaves, then return to his cell and start plaiting the leaves to make a thick rope. He continued to do this for quite some time, until finally one night he got up very late, quietly tied the rope around a doorpost, then threw the rope over the nine metre high wall. He carried only a little food and water, and an old axe head. He climbed quickly and was soon over the other side of the wall, where he felt freed from his long imprisonment. He then directed his steps towards Fr Mina's cave.

When the Fathers noticed his absence the following day, they were certain that he had fled using the rope that was dangling from the monastery's wall. They told the Abbot, who in turn told them, "Father Abd el-Mesih el-Habashi will not last long without enough water. He will surely return for more water in a few days, and when he does, we will capture him and quickly shut the gates." This exact thing happened later; he returned, knocked on the door and asked for food and drink. When the other monks opened the gates, they appeared to serve him, but then forbade him from leaving again.

He tried his old plan again with the rope, and he again escaped to his cell. When the Fathers saw that he had not listened to their advice, they called the police, who came and escorted Father Abd el-Mesih to the monastery, tied up with ropes. They forced him to take a pledge in front of everyone that he would not leave the monastery again, and explained to him the dangers of leaving, due to his being an Ethiopian citizen. As a result, however, he felt bitter about the Abbot's actions.

This was the beginning of his trials and troubles, but there is no doubt he knew that the road would be arduous and full of temptation. He also knew that these temptations would become blessing, joy and consolation. His readings of the *Sayings of the Desert Fathers*, and his extreme love for the ascetic life of Saint Isaac (whose writings he kept with him) helped. Father Abd el-Mesih to decide to leave the monastery and go to live in a cave, regardless of any hardship that might come upon him.

So he left for the third time, not out of disobedience (for they did not prohibit him for any spiritual reason, nor because he had not attained a suitable level of spirituality), but as a kind of protection of a foreigner monk especially that Father Abd el-Mesih when he came from Ethiopia, he did not have any official identification. Had anything happen to him especially at the time of war, the monastery would be held responsible.

At this point, the Abbot sent a message directly to the His Holiness Pope Youannes the nineteenth, and told him what had happened, and that he was no longer responsible for Father Abd el-Mesih el-Habashi's welfare. The Pope calmed him down, and advised him to leave Father Abd el-Mesih alone. These events took place in June of 1936.

TWO

....

The Beginning of His Struggle

FATHER ABD EL-MESIH EL-HABASHI went to live in the cell previously occupied by Father Mina of the Baramous, which also previously belonged to Rev Father Sarabamoun of the Baramous, the late Abbot of that Monastery. (He left the cell in 1925 and it then became the dwelling place of Mina the monk).

Its dimensions were about 4 metres by 2 metres, with the longer side facing the east. However, due to rocks pressing against its walls, its dimensions shrank to about 2 metres by 2 metres, and of course it did not have a door. In 1992 a metal gate was installed for protection.

After a few months, Father Abd el-Mesih el-Habashi moved further away from the monastery. He went out and searched the desert until he found a large rock about 2.8 kilometres away from the monastery. He then started carving beneath the rock in a non-architectural manner, and made a hole at the other end for ventilation. He also left his new cell without the protection of a door, taking his idea from the beasts of the desert, who had no doors for their dens.

According to the sayings of the elderly Fathers of the Monastery, he would place two palm branches at the door of the cell, positioned in the shape of a cross. Ismael, who was the chauffeur at the Ethiopian Embassy, also recounts that when he was escorted to Father Abd el-Mesih el-Habashi's cell by a fellow monk from the monastery, (possibly the late Rev Father Yacoub of the Baramous), accompanied by two metropolitans from Ethiopia, Father Abd el-Mesih had placed two palm branches at his door. When he was called outside, he put the leaves aside and went to greet them.

In his book *The Monasteries and The Monks in The Deserts*, Professor Otto Meinardus said that Rev Father Antonios el-Suriany (His Holiness Pope Shenouda III) pleaded with Father Abd el-Mesih to place a door to his cell, but his calm response was, "I am a wolf...I am like a wolf, and a wolf does not put a door on its den."

I have heard of an incident, which was described in the book *The Paradise of the Monks* as follows: one of the elderly monks was walking in the presence of another monk and as they passed by the cell of Saint Anthony, he pointed to the cell and sighed, saying, "Behold, a lion living as a wolf in this cell." According to this saying, the lion is Saint Anthony, however we are not sure whether he meant that the wolf was a real wolf, or that a person who had the personality of a wolf was living in that cell! Father Abd el-Mesih el-Habashi had the characteristics of a lion in his courage and long-suffering, for he lived as a lion, in what looked like a wolf's den, as His Holiness Pope Shenouda III described him.

Now Let Us Go and Visit Him in His Cell

Out of courtesy, we would take him something by way of blessing, such as some dry beans. We would also have to travel around 3 kilometres west of the monastery, on a daring mission in the dry desert heat, on an untamed path, with prickly cacti here and there, and the sun beating down on us, with the wind carrying the familiar and beloved smell of the sand.

We must remember to ensure that what we are wearing is not expensive, and preferably dirty looking, in case Father Abd el-Mesih el-Habashi sees us. We should also have our walking staffs with us.

From a distance, Father Abd el-Mesih el-Habashi is becoming discernable above a small hill. As we draw near him, he sees us and quickly scrambles down from the top of the cell, and goes quickly inside. He emerges again as we almost close in on the site of his cell. To our surprise, he has been wrapping himself with a blanket to cover his nakedness.

However, once he sees us, he rejoices greatly, and bows down to us. His Arabic words are very few, sparse and not related. As we start to sit, he quickly goes to the front of the cell and dusts off a place for us to sit on. He then rushes inside and comes back with dried bread.

He goes inside yet again to bring us a carton of

olives. He continues to do so, very light and quick on his feet, and every time he goes inside, he emerges with a new type of food: beans, lentils... "Eat, my Fathers... eat...this is YOUR food." Father Abd el-Mesih el-Habashi also gives us money.

He is very comical, yet at the same time we are deeply moved, as this comedy is mixed with the presence of an incredible human being, rare and so loving, but why does he do all this?

Rev Father Mina el-Baramousy (currently) said that out of his curious nature, he wanted to see for himself what was inside Father Abd el-Mesih el-Habashi's cell, so one day he quickly ran into in his cell unannounced. To his surprise, he could only see his bed, made of dried palm leaves, a blanket, and two or three books in a corner.

"Even though the place was dark and humid, and was so constricted that I could not turn around freely, it was completely filled with a mysterious, enigmatic secret! There was a holy and blessed breath of air in it, which took me back centuries in time, and I felt the clock turning back, until it felt like the fourth century," Rev Father Mina el-Baramousy said.

Allow me to interrupt this narrative to tell an important story. His Grace Bishop Makarious the Ethiopian said that he visited Father Abd el-Mesih el-Habashi when he was just a monk known by the name Botros el-Suriany (from el-Surian monastery). "I entered Father Abd el-Mesih el-Habashi's cell to take a look inside, but all I found was the blanket he slept under, a rag that he probably slept on top of, a book of Psalms and another book, but the walls were empty of any pictures of saints or verses from the Bible. "I went outside with a new outlook towards Father Abd el-Mesih el-Habashi and sat down quietly next to him, listening to his conversation with another fellow monk. "He talked about the lives of some saints in a few Arabic words, and mentioned some facts about the ecumenical councils.

"We then ate some food, and he insisted that we take more, but we politely refused. He then further insisted that we take the little money he had, but we did not accept it, and we calmed him down. As we were getting ready to leave, and asked him to pray for us, he gently said in the simplest way ever, "I am a donkey...I am a donkey...Please pray for me in your cells."

"We left his cell with amazement and sympathy. We walked on for about 100 metres, when we turned back to look at him, to find him standing facing the East, raising his hands in prayer. It seemed that he was accustomed to praying for anyone who asked him, so that God may bless them." After leaving Father Abd el-Mesih, Rev Father Markos el-Sabky turned to see him praying.

Doctor Nazeeh Asad (an engineer at the University of Alexandria) said that when he visited Father Abd el-Mesih for the first time ever, he found him wearing tattered clothes, and a white scarf tied on his head, and holding a blanket around him that covered almost all of his body. He would never let anyone kiss his hands, but would bow down to anyone who bowed down to him. He used to sit cross legged on the ground in front of his cell when visitors came to him.

His Way of Life

When asked by some of the Fathers how he spent his day, Father Abd el-Mesih el-Habashi responded with the usual monastic response, "A little prayer...a little reading...a little work." In his humility, Father Abd el-Mesih el-Habashi's 'little' prayer is actually a lot. The actual things he ever had little of were food and rest at night.

In the first documented life of Father Abd el-Mesih by Bishop Dioscorus of el-Monofeya in the year 1960; who knew him personally relates that "he used to spend a lot time with in his cell, seldom coming out of it. He used to spend most of his day reading and researching, to the extent that he had been seen reading by moonlight at night."

In terms of literal knowledge, he used to like reading the Holy Bible, stories of the saints and martyrs, the history of the church, and the ecumenical councils, which were the three main topics he would raise with his loving visitors. Whoever met him outside his cell would witness his great knowledge of the Bible and the stories of the saints; he would surprise his visitors by telling them the name of the saint of the day, and the saint's life story, along with his explanation of the heresies and his response to them.

One day Father Saweros el-Baramousy visited Father Abd el-Mesih on the commemoration of St. Saweros of Antioch. Father Abd el-Mesih started telling him how St Saweros had once attended a church in disguise, and how the holy bread for the offertory kept disappearing. The priest of the church then discovered that this Pope was present in the church.

Father Tadros el-Baramousy tells the story that one day Father Abd el-Mesih el-Habashi explained the details of the heresy of Mani, and the church's response to it. In a rare recording, Father Abd el-Mesih was recorded explaining the Trinity to Rev Father Anastasy el-Samuel and other Fathers in Arabic.

His manual labour consisted of his knitting palm

leaves to make little baskets, which he would use to store bread for monks. In slang, this basket was called 'bakoota.' He would also knit loofahs to make ropes. He usually sent the ropes to the monastery for general use, and would bring any new monk a new bread basket.

Sometimes he would start knitting a basket on his way from his cell to the monastery, and would finish it by the time he reached the door of the monastery, leaving it for one of the Fathers as a blessing.

Father Mansour el-Baramousy said that unlike the norm, Father Abd el-Mesih el-Habashi would start knitting the basket from top to bottom! On the other hand, his ropes were of a very high quality. This same thing was verified by Hagg Ghayora in Wadi el-Natroun, who said that the ropes that were made by Father Abd el-Mesih looked like the ones made mechanically by machines.

His Prayer

We know that prayer is the measure of one's spiritual life, for if a person's prayer is shallow and brief, we know that he is spiritually weak, but if his prayers are deep, then his spiritual level is also deep. We also know that prayer is the translation of the love deeply rooted inside our hearts towards God. Father Abd el-Mesih el-Habashi could not be spiritually strong if he were not a man of prayer. A large portion of his day was spent in prayer.

Father Philoxinus el-Suriany, who visited him repeatedly, tells us a story that once happened to him when he visited Father Abd el-Mesih unexpectedly. He was gently reprimanded by our holy Father, as it appeared that he was on a higher spiritual level at that time, and did not want to be disturbed by a human. He also says that Father Abd el-Mesih knew the hundred and fifty one Psalms by heart.

This incident happened again, but this time Father Abd el-Mesih signalled for Father Philoxinus to sit down while he went to finish what he was doing. Obviously he was praying, and this happened many times with this Father. Bishop Makarious the Ethiopian said that Father Abd el-Mesih knew all his prayers; he did not need a book to assist him.

His Grace Bishop Isaac (Father Wissa el-Suriany at that time) recounts that when he went to Father Abd el-Mesih's cell to take him in his Jeep to go to the monastery for treatment, Father Abd el-Mesih told him in all seriousness, "A monk has a rule of prayer that he needs to fulfil before he can leave his cell," and he turned towards the East, and started prostrating many times, for over fifteen minutes in the blazing sun, spending this time in deep and powerful prayer, while bowing down in the sand.

As was mentioned before, he would stand atop his cell and pray to God after his visitors left him, so that God would bless his visitors, and also because his visitors would request Father Abd el-Mesih el-Habashi to pray for them.

When he lived in a room in the Papal residence, before leaving Egypt for Jerusalem, one of the servants of the church of Anba Reweis said that when he was still a young child, he looked over through the gap at the top of the door and saw Father Abd el-Mesih el-Habashi huddled in a corner of the room, holding a rosary in his hands, and praying in a style of extreme spiritual elevation - called 'hazeez' in Arabic – which denotes continual prayer to God. So the child fled, scared of what he had seen.

His Asceticism

Father Abd el-Mesih el-Habashi was widely known by his beloved and others for the great ascetic life that he led. What we are really interested in is not the many stories that outline his asceticism, but rather his philosophy of life and his revulsion towards the world and desire.

Here I would like to recount the very first witness by a Protestant writer, Otto Meinardus, who wrote two books about monasteries and monks in Egypt, one in German, and the other in English. It is important to note that this writer, who died in 2005, does not believe in monasticism like all other Protestants; thus his witness is of great importance in this matter.

In his book written in English, he pointed out that twice when he visited Father Abd el-Mesih el-Habashi, he was deeply astonished by Father's peaceable nature towards the world. He requested to leave him some food, but Father Abd el-Mesih el-Habashi refused, saying that he would give it to passers-by. He then said to him, "God gives me food each day, hence you should not feed me of your own food!"

Furthermore, Meinardus says, "When I tried to convince him to eat more, due to his ill shaped face and deteriorating health, he answered joyfully saying, 'When I am ill, God will protect me and bless me even more, and I do not ask for more than that.'"

Saint Isaac the Syrian says, "Whoever is not concerned about temporal things, but leaves everything to God night and day without worrying about any worldly matters, departing from them to experience heavenly matters, is no longer troubled by fulfilling his bodily needs of food and clothes. He does not care where he will lay his body to rest, but rests in the hope that God will truly care for him, because he fully believes that He will prepare his needs; this is the real and wise hope.

"This man has the right to put his hope in the Lord, because he has become His servant, concerned only about his salvation without delay, regardless of reason, and he has the right to show God his sincere concern in a special way, for he knows His commandment which says: 'But seek first the kingdom of God and His righteousness, and all these things shall be added to you' (Matthew 6:33). All the world then becomes his own bondservant, listens to him, refuses none of his requests, and does not question his will. Such a person is not disrupted by his bodily needs; therefore his continual presence with God is not interrupted. Out of his fear of God, he is not concerned about any other thing, as little or big as it may be, which he knows would drive him towards lust. He knows full well that he will receive all his needs in miraculous ways, without his being concerned over them."

Thus, Father Abd el-Mesih el-Habashi's asceticism protects him and fills him with the correct, spiritual conscience, teaching him to fully depend on God who granted him life. In order to try to pressure him to return to live with them again, the Fathers deprived him of bread for a few days. So he managed to collect all the bread crumbs he had, and some onion leaves, mixed them with water and grilled them on a fire. Eating this caused him intense abdominal pain, and brought dire illness to his whole body, to the extent that worms emerged from his stomach, so he was forced to go to a doctor.

From then on, all of the monks were very sympathetic toward him, and pitied him more than before, to a degree that worried and greatly upset him, so much so that he personally stated to the above mentioned Dr. Meinardus that the monks of el-Baramous and el-Surian monasteries had waged war against him, and that this was due to their pressuring him to pay attention to his food.

His usual meal was made up of bread and olives, and some beans and lentils. He would walk to the monastery once a week to get two thirds of a barrel of water and some beans and lentils. Rev Father Tadrous el-Baramousy said that Father Abd el-Mesih would take extra bread with him to give to the Arab Bedouins who would exchange bread for firewood with Father

Abd el-Mesih so that he could use it as fuel.

Rizk Iskander (of Kom Hamada) saw Father Abd el-Mesih waiting outside the monastery's gate for his food and water. When Father Yacoub came out with bread, onion and the barrel of water, Father Abd el-Mesih took the bread and onion and placed them inside his garments, as he was girded with leather on the outside. He then took off his headband and put it inside his clothes, took out another piece of cloth, which he shaped into a ring, put on his head and placed the barrel of water on it. He then set off and started walking to his cell. When Rizk tried to offer his help, he refused.

Rev. Father Mansour el-Baramousy said that he would pour cooked lentils on a plastic bag to dry them, and then tie up the bag after beating its contents to powder, so that he could use a little of it, adding boiling water as needed for food to eat during his only daily meal at sunset.

Father Youssef el-Mahreky, who was with Father Abd el-Mesih during his first years in the monastery, said that he used to see him sneak up to the kitchen, collect leftover or rotten lentils, dry them and mix them with salt to preserve them to start his life of solitude in the cell.

His only meal took place at sunset, and he had a truly unusual way of eating, as he would mix different kinds of food together, most of which would already have expired, then eat them. He abstained from meat and fish, as well as all dairy products such as milk, cheese and eggs. He did not eat any vegetables until the end of his life, when strongly advised by doctors to do so.

Father Armeya el-Baramousy recounts that once he brought Father Father Abd el-Mesih some fish from the Monastery, as this was the main food served on that day, but he refused to eat it, so he had to return to the Monastery with it.

Bishop Isaac recounts that once Father Abd el-Mesih el-Habashi got lost in a sandstorm. Afterwards he spotted el-Surian Monastery and he quickly went toward it. When the Fathers sensed his presence, they went out to meet him, and when he sat down to eat, they offered him a can of sardines, which he refused to eat, saying that he did not eat meat so they offered him a plate of lentils. He agreed to eat it after mixing the lentils with bread and tea!

Meinardus recounts in his book that he went to Father Abd el-Mesih one day, accompanied by the late Rev Father Mattias el-Baramousy. Father Mattias was carrying some cans of sardines to give to him, however he refused and reproached him severely, and forced him to carry the sardines back with him. Father Abd el-Mesih el-Habashi personally told Meinardus that such food can be harmful to a monk.

Rev Father Yousab el-Suriany recounts that when Father Abd el-Mesih's health deteriorated, he accompanied him to a doctor, along with a layperson called Erian Iskander (now in Canada).

On their way back from the doctor's, Erian invited him over to his house, and hosted him generously by setting up a table full of all types of food. When Father Abd el-Mesih sat down to eat, he asked him about each type of food and its name. There was meat, fish, vegetables, rice, and other delicacies, but after they told him the name of the dish, he would order them to take it away, until the only thing remaining on the table was a dish of salad!

We know that in the Coptic monastic tradition, asceticism is not about totally ignoring the body and forbidding it its needs, for we should give the flesh what it needs to nourish it, according to the laws set in the Holy Bible: 'but nourishes and cherishes it' (Ephesians 5:29). We are taught that the body is a gift that we must protect, so that the body can serve us in our struggles, from the struggle of prayer, to staying up at night, to prostrations, and handling periods of fasting. However, in the days in which fasting is prohibited, we allow the body to cross that line slightly, but only to a certain extent, so that I discipline my body and bring it into subjection (1 Corinthians 9:27).

Father Philoxinus el-Suriany agrees that Father Abd el-Mesih would eat a full meal (that is, his meal met all of his nutritional needs), however without any taste, so that he could kill the body's lust for food. He used food only as a means to keep him alive.

He offered his visitors the best of his food, however his best was distasteful. When His Grace Bishop Makarious the Ethiopian would visit him, he would offer him some hot water, sprinkled with chilli flakes and sugarcane syrup on top!

Rizk Iskander says that he was on a trip with about another twenty visitors to Father Abd el-Mesih. "He offered us a large plate of grapes and pleaded with us to take from it, so we reluctantly did, pained by the fact that we were eating his food. We later found out from the accompanying monk that Father Abd el-Mesih did not eat grapes, and that previous visitors had brought him those grapes."

Father Tawadrous el-Suriany also recounts that Father Mina el-Suriany the monk wanted to visit Father Abd el-Mesih el-Habashi, so he lived next to him for five days, during which Father Abd-el Mesih would offer him a little water with molokheya, chilli flakes and halawa after cooking these on the fire.

In his extreme daily asceticism, Father Abd el-Mesih also personally recounted to Father Armeya el-Baramousy of the tedious times that he lived through, having little to no food or drink, as he would be very generous with Arab Bedouins, who would visit him often.

Father Armeya el Baramousy says that when Father Abd el-Mesih told him about this, he comforted him and consoled his spirit by saying that this was nothing but wars from Satan, who envied his love for Christ. On hearing this, he would become extremely joyful, and his face shone with a mysterious light.

However, the Arabs and the camel herders, along with people living in surrounding districts of Wadi el-Natroun, who befriended Father Abd el-Mesih, would visit him, carrying food out of their love for him. He would accept it all with an open heart and great joy, but would eventually give it to others.

Meinardus recounts the story when Father Abd el-Mesih el-Habashi was forced to go to a doctor in Alexandria. The doctor prescribed suitable nutritional food for him in order to strengthen his weakened body; however he took the food and gave it all to the driver who was taking him back to the monastery.

Mr Naeem Tadrous has another story, which runs along these same lines: he visited Father Abd el-Mesih in his cell with other people. The monk presented a plate full of beans, okra, zucchini and eggplant! The visitors exchanged looks of surprise, but when the monk noticed their looks, he offered them a plate of fruit, which other people had previously brought him. Mr Naeem explains that he later found out that Father Abd el-Mesih would mix all his food so that it would lose its taste and pleasant flavours. This is a model for every person who goes to great lengths to perfect their food's flavours.

Rev Father Mansour el-Baramousy adds that Father Abd el-Mesih was accustomed to eating a handful of chillies every now and then! This was not done for pleasure; on the contrary: he used to do it so that he might train his stomach to tolerate it. This was also his way of cleansing his insides of any microbes that might have entered through eating any rotten food.

His Use of Money

Father Abd el-Mesih el-Habashi used to make baskets and ropes out of palm leaves, and then sell them to Arabs for little money. He would not, however, keep this money with him in his cell, but would give it out to his visitors as soon as he could. His hand made products were of a very high quality, to the extent that four baskets have been preserved till this day: two in the monastery, and two with a man called Rizk Iskander.

Dr Ragheb Moftah tells the story that Father Abd el-Mesih went to the Papal residency to beg the Pope to allow him to visit Jerusalem. The Pope allowed him to stay in a room to rest, and gave him forty pounds, which at the time was a huge amount of money. However, Father Abd el-Mesih gave it all away to the people working in the residency, saying, "How can I leave forty devils to spend the night with me tonight?!!"

His Use of Water

As recounted by the elderly Fathers of the monastery, Father Abd el-Mesih el-Habashi would fill a twenty litre can with water and use it every week. He would end up drinking only about 15 litres because the rest of the water would spill from the tin can on the way to his cell. It is, however, known that the average daily water usage for a human being is about ten litres per day. Hence he would save his water, to the extent that would extend this period to longer than a week.

He would put his water in a clay jar which was fixed to the ground. However, the jar was prone to access by insects which would fall in the water, as well as to dust and mud.

Saad Mettias (of Tela) recounts that once when he was on one of his visits to Father Abd el-Mesih, he went behind his back to drink from the clay jar. However Father Abd el-Mesih caught him and stopped him, saying, "This will break your stomach!" But when Saad asked him how he drinks it, he said, "I am a donkey!!!" Keep in mind that the water was green and full of algae.

On the other hand, Father Armeya el-Baramousy said that when he brought water in a can to Father Abd el-Mesih, a lot of the water was spilled on the way to his cell. He got upset because he knew that Father Abd el-Mesih would have to drink a lot less for the whole week because of his mistake. However, when Father Abd el-Mesih saw that there was little water, he had compassion on Father Armeya and told him, "The water is little, but it is enough, do not be upset, do not worry…it is more than enough." When Father Armeya looked at him questioningly, having pity on him, Father Abd el-Mesih replied sternly saying, "You do not know God (as in His support)." He would say this a lot when people would pity his hard and deserted life, full of troubles and low on food or water.

Rev Father Yousab el-Suriany said that once a novice monk wanted to stay over in his cell, and Father

Abd el-Mesih agreed, which is very unusual. This monk was either not serious in his request, or was not familiar with the hard life of asceticism. On the first day, Father Abd el-Mesih poured out some water in a very filthy plate, and by the end of the first day, the water had changed in colour. On the second day, the water began to smell, and by the third day the smell was unbearable, and only then did he drink it. At that point the monk could not continue, and left to make his way back to the Surian Monastery.

When Father Abd el-Mesih used to drink tea, he would put salt in it instead of sugar. When he would accept visitors for only a few minutes, they would insist that he drink tea, so he would ask for salt with his tea. They initially thought he did not know the difference between the words sugar and salt, so they thought he did not know what he was saying, but as he repeated the same request many times, they started to realise that he was fully conscious of his demand. We must clarify that in Ethiopia, salt was one of the most expensive import items, and only wealthy people would use it. They would add salt to visitors' drinks as a way of honouring them.

Salt was extracted in Ethiopia, in the province of Dello, the province that the country follows; this is also where Father Abd el-Mesih was born. However the government would control salt sales, exports and extraction.

Due to his great ascetic life, his health deteriorated to a great extent. At one stage, when he had a medical check-up in Alexandria, the doctor stated that Father Abd el-Mesih's stomach had shrunk to the size of a three year old child's. The only way that he could ever survive was if he were to eat a lot of vegetables.

However, despite his nature, he agreed to eat

whatever vegetables he was able to gather, such as lettuce, rocket and the like, and would call them 'hasheesh' (grass) as slang. He would reach the stage of severe constipation before being compel into eating vegetables.

Showering

Rev. Father Tadrous el-Baramousy, along with Father Sawirus el-Baramousy, agree on the fact that when Father Abd el-Mesih wanted to shower, he would go and knock at the monastery gate and ask to fill his can of water, then would take it to an empty room next to the gates of the monastery, and pour the water on his body. After a few minutes he would come back and ask to fill his can of water again, but he would take it back to his cell. This would happen about once every few weeks.

Rev Father Youssab el Suriany tells a similar story; he says that Father Abd el-Mesih once went to the Surian Monastery, and sat on the garden fence. He asked for a bucket of water, which he poured on his head as he sat there!

Father Tadrous el-Baramousy, Father Mansour el-Baramousy and Father Youssab el-Suriany all witnessed this and said that despite this practice, his body was very clean and, probably due to his great asceticism, lacked any fat.

George Tesphary of Ethiopia agreed: when he visited him in his room in the Papal residence, he kissed his hand. He says that he did not smell anything suspicious; on the contrary, he had a pleasant aroma. The chauffeur of the Ethiopian embassy, Ismael, says that he was in the presence of two Ethiopian bishops visiting Father Abd el-Mesih and he kissed his hand,

and his aroma was very pleasant.

His clothes

And having food and clothing, with these we shall be content.

- 1 TIMOTHY 6:8

We have previously said that Father Abd el-Mesih had every one of his simple needs fulfilled. He did not struggle to become an ascetic monk, for virtues are not goals in the life of strugglers; their one and only goal is to unite their minds with God. All other virtues are the effects caused by such an important goal. Father Abd el-Mesih did not struggle to keep himself from anything; he was too busy to worry about his food!

In my opinion, he did not intentionally wait for his food to go rotten, but he was so busy that he forgot his food, until bacteria infected him. Due to his leading an ascetic life, and his discontent with food, rotten food was pleasant and acceptable to him!

We know that God interacts with His children in two ways, or on two levels:

The first: Fulfilling their needs.

The second: Reducing their needs.

This simply means that God provides the needs of novice monks, and fulfils their requirements, whilst stripping away the needs and requirements of older, highly spiritual people, so that they do not need a thing!

This brings our attention to Father Abd el-Mesih's clothes. He would wear one overall to cover his nakedness when he was in the company of visitors, or when he would visit the monastery, or on rare occasions when he left the monastery.

Most of his visitors agree on this: that when they used to visit him, they would find him standing naked in front of his cell. When he sensed them approaching, he would quickly run into his cell and cover himself with a blanket.

It was told that he was seen wearing a white piece of cloth around himself, and he used to wear a white headband of simple cotton.

It is mentioned in the book of the matters concerning Ethiopian monasticism, that thousands upon thousands of monks and nuns would hold in their hands a long wooden staff, atop which is a bronze or silver cross. They would also wear white headbands of soft cloth, like the cloth used by Egyptians.

Father Filexinus el-Suriany says that he saw Father Abd el-Mesih naked twice; the first time when he was sitting cross legged knitting palm leaves, and the second time when he came out of his cell completely naked. The moment he saw him, he ran inside and covered himself with anything – most of the time it would be a single blanket. We will see in the following pages how he used to view his body parts in a holy manner.

Father Armeya el-Baramous says that Father Abd el-Mesih probably had two reasons for him to be naked. The first is that he is denying his body of its normal bodily covering or protection. The other reason is that he had no need to cover himself, except in front of others of course.

Whenever anyone would give him new clothes, he would reject them. Those who knew about this tried to offer him worn out and torn pieces of garments. He only accepted these when he was indeed in need of them.

Father Filexinus, who would visit Father Abd el-

Mesih frequently, said that he had two garments which smelled terrible; he had probably not changed them for decades.

This was also witnessed by Meinardus, in his German book: when Rev Father Mattias el Baramous visited Father Abd el-Mesih with him, his clothes were worn out and torn.

Dr Ragheb Moftah recounts that Pope Youannes the Nineteenth, Pope of Alexandria, visited the Baramous Monastery, accompanied by Emperor Haile Selassie. The emperor left Father Abd el-Mesih an expensive piece of wool in the monastery. The monks told Father Abd el-Mesih that it was a gift from Dr Ragheb Moftah – who loved him very much – and asked him to accept it. Father Abd el-Mesih almost accepted it, were it not for a monk who told him the truth. So Father Abd el-Mesih took the wool and cut it into pieces with scissors.

Due to this incident, he had an extreme dislike for people who wore expensive clothes, especially monks or bishops, who are in fact monks. He would show his serious disapproval in a comic way.

When Bishop Thaofilus - who later became the Ethiopian pope – visited him after being ordained a bishop, Father Abd el-Mesih criticised him severely for wearing expensive clothes. This incident was repeated again with the late Bishop Benjamin of el-Monofeya (as was recounted by Rev Father Tawadrous el-Suriany).

Rev Father Yousab el-Suriany says that when he visited the Baramous Monastery to take the blessings of Bishop Makarious, the other monks warned him repeatedly not to make any comment about monastic clothes, and Father Abd el-Mesih promised. However, the moment he saw him, he criticised him.

The honorable Mr Banoub Shehata (of Los Angeles)

recounts that when Father Abd el-Mesih el-Habashi left Egypt to visit Jerusalem, he rested for some time in Amman. Metropolitan Basilius of Jerusalem visited him, so he signalled that he should sit beside him. When the Metropolitan took a seat beside him on the ground, he started criticising him, saying, "Are you not a monk?" He said, "Yes." So he replied saying, "Then why do you wear expensive clothes?" Metropolitan Basilius was quiet for a long time as he sat beside him on the floor.

He had his own philosophy on this subject, for he saw that softness of clothes is not among the characteristics of a monk, but rather that a true monk is one who rejects all materialistic aspects of life, even his basic needs and requirements. This was done so that a monk might live up to the sayings of the ancient desert Fathers about the clothes of a monk: that if they were left outside a cell for three days, nobody would even bother looking at them.

Importantly, Father Abd el-Mesih the Ethiopian was amazed by the simplicity of the clothes of both Father Antonious el-Suriany (Pope Shenouda III) and the late Bishop Thaofilus, the Abbot of the Surian Monastery. They both would wear simple clothes, and hold a wooden stick in their hands. This could very well be the reason why he loved them dearly.

At the same time, he was not bothered by the fact that a monk accepted to be ordained a bishop, except that becoming a bishop meant that the monk would have to take care of how he looks and how he eats, and what his possessions are. In Father Abd el-Mesih's view, being a bishop is, at some level, free of any monastic life as a rite.

His Personal Tools

Only the simplest things belonged to Father Abd el-Mesih. He had a worn out bed of palm branches, and one well worn blanket. He had a can of water (15 litre capacity) which he used to bring water from the monastery. He also had a little, old plate, which he used to carry whatever he brought from the monastery to cook, and a broken clay jar inside which he would light a fire, and some firewood.

When we cleaned his cell, we found little holes in the bottom of the walls, like rats' nests. We were told that he used to keep the little bread he had inside them. At the entrance to his cell lay a few palm branches and fibres, which he used to make ropes by hand (as was previously explained). From time to time, he needed a shovel to level out the sand, and an axe to cut his firewood. Thus, the monastery kept some of these tools, as well as a blanket, which still had some bread crumbs clinging to it, from the food Father Abd el-Mesih used to eat. Two revered elderly Fathers kept two baskets made by Father Abd el-Mesih, and Bishop Isaac kept a hat that he used to wear. Rev. Father Yousab kept the shovel and axe. Furthermore, another Father kept another hat which he used to wear, a piece of a blanket and a spoon. We previously mentioned that Father Abd el-Mesih kept the book of Psalms written in Tigrinya (even though he knew it like the back of his hand), the book *ascetical homilies of St Isaac the Saint* in the same language, and the Holy Bible.

Wars Within His Cell

The first trial that faced Father Abd el-Mesih was the monastery's refusal to allow him to live alone.

They pressured him to return against his will, but he never doubted his path. He put in his heart that both St Anthony and St Macarius had gone to the desert, roaming about its plane, and God never left them alone. He might have told himself, "Even if I die here from beasts or from hunger, at least I will have perished for the sake of Christ, and this would be martyrdom to me."

Truth be told, Father Abd el-Mesih was martyred one drop of blood at a time, over a period of 50 years, which marked his extreme asceticism that none other could match. He told the stories of his sufferings to Bishop Macarius the Ethiopian; these include one where an army soldier came to him in his cell and started abusing him for living alone. However Father Abd el-Mesih replied saying, "Am I a thief? Or a murderer? Am I a troublemaker? Then why don't you leave me alone?" So the soldier apologised and left him.

Many Fathers of the Monastery of the Surian and other priests tell of the famous story that happened to him. During the Second World War, as Lieutenant Rumel was wandering the western desert, some soldiers noticed a faint light shining from a little crack in the desert landscape. They thought it was a German spy, so they opened fire on him, but God's protection covered him, so that he was not hurt by any stray bullet. The army soldiers approached the source of the light, only to see a lonely Ethiopian man. When they asked him who he was, they didn't understand him because Father Abd el-Mesih spoke in Arabic. He tried desperately to tell them that he was only a monk from the Baramous Monastery. They only picked up the word Baramous, so they left to go to the monastery to find out who he was. The monks calmed them down and assured them he was only a simple monk living in solitude in the mountain, so they left him alone. However, according to Meinardus, the soldiers offered Father Abd el-Mesih and the monastery some services.

He never tired of telling all his visitors the story of how the bullets went around his head, but never struck him. He even kept some of the bullet shells in his cell until he left it. He also told of the tin plates in the sky (he meant aeroplanes), and the lights dangling from them. This story incidentally forced Father Abd el-Mesih to go to the Ethiopian Embassy in Egypt to obtain proof that he was an Ethiopian monk.

Other spiritual warfares that he faced included the deserted nature of the place, and the widespread presence of crawling creatures and wild beasts. However, the Lord gave him authority over all creatures, so he lived peacefully with them.

We wonder, how such a man could live in a very inhospitable environment, in a land that was not his own, whose language he did not speak, and if he needed something, how could he get it? How could he live in a desolate cave, with no door or window, and furthermore, how could he live without support?

He had tremendous faith that God would never leave him. He would always reply to pitying comments from visitors, "There is Ekhristous," that is, God is present. God rewarded such faith by rewarding him more than any other monk, as He accepted his full reliance on Him, so He sheltered him from harm.

When one of the elderly Fathers asked him about solitude so that he may also practise it, Father Abd el-Mesih would reply with a hint of pity and despair saying, "Think…a lot…a lot…a lot!!" This meant that he had experienced a lot of tribulations via his thoughts, wondering whether he should carry on living in solitude.

Father Tadrous el-Baramousy informs us that Father Abd el-Mesih faced a miserable war of thoughts, where he would be fought with desires to such a great extent that many times he would leave his cell, go to the monastery and ask the other monks to pray for him. He was never embarrassed by revealing these thoughts to them.

THREE

BETWEEN CELL AND CHURCH

WHEN FATHER ABD EL-MESIH EL-HABASHI came to the monastery every Saturday morning, he would ring the bell, and would greet whoever opened the door and hand him his tin can of water to fill up. However, the Fathers who knew he was coming would await him at the door to talk to him about different issues and ask him questions. He would happily spend hours on end with them, but would then take the tin can of water and some food and go back to his cell. He would strongly reject any offers of help to return to his cell. If no one waited for him at the gate, he would simply fill his water can, take his food and return silently to his cell.

The few times he was forced to stay overnight in the monastery, he would refuse to sleep in a cell, but rather would sleep on a pile of hay inside the front gate. If the monks insisted otherwise, or refused to allow him to sleep like that, he also would insist, trying to explain himself with the few Arabic words he knew.

However the Fathers that used to visit him often all agreed on the fact that he was very generous and gentle towards them. He would be extremely joyous when they visited him, and would lovingly exhort them. When they visited, he would start talking to them about the saint of the day and his life story. He would talk about all matters concerning monasticism and the church, and how it should return to its original state.

The Fathers of the Surian Monastery

When Father Bacillius el-Baramous, the abbot of the monastery, forbade his life of solitude, it made him bitter, which made him all the more ready to leave and go to the Surian Monastery. Whenever he would feel restricted by the monastery, he would ask for little things…

Bishop Theophilus had compassion on Father Abd el-Mesih, and would visit him many times, carrying with him whatever he could; he was the person that suggested making a door for his cell, which he refused (as was mentioned before).

Father Antonious el-Suriany also used to visit him, staying with him for days to talk to him and listen to him, for he was fond of him. In the times that he would go to the Surian Monastery to gather his food, the late Bishop Theophilus assigned Father Botrous el Suriany

(Bishop Macarius the Ethiopian) to go to Father Abd el-Mesih's cell, carrying his food and water on a donkey. At some point, he assigned that job to Father Wissa el-Suriany (currently Bishop Isaac). This coincided with the visitations of many other monks from both the Surian and the Baramous monasteries. They waged a war against him to leave his ascetic life due to his deteriorating health.

Bishop Macarius the Ethiopian says that his relationship with Father Abd el-Mesih began in 1951, when Bishop Theophilus sent him to carry Father Abd el-Mesih his food (beans, lentils and molasses) either on foot or on a donkey, and he would take the route through the Baramous Monastery.

He also recounts that Father Abd el-Mesih el-Habashi visited the Surian Monastery at that time, and the Fathers at the monastery wanted to wash his feet, so he accepted it as a Coptic and Ethiopian custom. When Father Botrous (Bishop Macarius) visited him, Father Abd el-Mesih wanted to wash his feet, but he refused saying, "You wash them with your tears" (pointing to the small amount of the water he had). Father Abd el-Mesih, however, insisted and said as a joke, "You are like Peter...Peter always refused to allow anyone to wash his feet," then he added, "I was silly when I let you wash my feet at the Surian Monastery."

He fell sick one day, and some of the youth who were going to the Surian Monastery found him and quickly informed the Fathers, who came and carried him to the monastery (according to the story by Bishop Isaac).

His Relationship with Visitors

The first of the laypeople to know Father Abd el-Mesih el-Habashi were the Bedouins who would pass by him, and he would have compassion on them. They in turn started talking about him to their friends in the region of Wadi el-Natroun, so that people would increasingly gather around him, longing for his blessings and words of wisdom, conveying their troubles and problems, and asking him for his prayers.

Besides this, many of these Bedouins are still alive and recall many stories about Father Abd el-Mesih.

Many of the shuttle bus drivers who brought visitors to Father Abd el-Mesih knew him very well, and knew the way to his cell. However as much as they loved him, they feared him too. Mr Rizk Iskander (of Koum Hamada) recalls that once he was driving a group of 20 visitors to see Father Abd el-Mesih, and on the way, he pleaded with the visitors not to become rowdy around his cell, and to keep silent and respect his presence, saying that he wanted to return safely home to his kids!

Father Macari Gad (of Tanta) tells the story of some teenagers in a four wheel drive who were passing by Father Abd el-Mesih's cave. They saw him and started mocking him and his appearance. Suddenly, the car stopped in its tracks and would not move. One of the passengers thought that this happened because they had mocked the saintly man, so they all walked up to him and pleaded his forgiveness. He forgave them, and the car started again of its own accord.

Many servants and youth from Cairo and surrounding regions knew the way to the holy Father, and would either go straight to his cell, or would go to the monastery and then visit him during their stay.

They tell countless stories, and they also became a main source of information about him. We have succeeded in collating information from sources all around Cairo, Alexandria, Tanta and Monoufeya.

Father Abd el-Mesih el-Habashi would talk to them at length, and offer them food, to the extent that some of his visitors had to sleep over near his cell because the sun had set and it was too late to leave. This may be the reason that he built a small room west of his personal cell, to receive visitors and Fathers. He was a great inspiration to many visitors, who later became his disciples and learned many things from him, and are very proud of it.

The closest person to Father Abd el-Mesih is apparently Dr Ragheb Moftah who says, "Father Abd el-Mesih el-Habashi joined the Baramous Monastery in the early 1930s, when I used to visit the monastery frequently. I learned a lot about him, and began to grow closer to him, and Father Abd el-Mesih began to like me more.

"Many a time I would visit him and he would tell me a list of the things he wanted me to bring down in my next visit, but people knew about this secret, and every visitor would bring something and say that it is from me. He would refuse to accept it, saying, "I did not ask him for any of these things." When the Fathers tried to explain to him that I had sent him a wool coat, which turned out to be from the Emperor of Ethiopia, he took scissors and cut it up." Moreover, Prof. Moftah had Father Abd el-Mesih stay in his house for three months until he left for Jerusalem.

His Relationship with Pope Kyrollos VI

The relationship between Father Abd el-Mesih el-Habashi and Pope Kyrollos VI began when Father Mina el-Baramousy was expelled from the monastery for showing sympathy to expelled monks, which led to him evacuating his cave. His cave was then occupied by Father Abd el-Mesih, as we mentioned earlier.

Rev Father Beimen el-Suriany reveals that when he was in the company of Father Abd el-Mesih with some visitors, and the vacant papal position was mentioned, he started saying, "The new pope is very good…the new pope is very good."

When Pope Kyrollos was chosen for the papal position, and came to visit the monastery with some bishops, Father Abd el-Mesih knew of his coming without anyone telling him. Everybody was surprised to see him come directly from his cell to where the Pope was staying. He was very angry, for he wanted to reprimand the Pope bitterly for leaving his rite of solitude and accepting the papal rank.

The late Pope Kyrollos knew in spirit about the coming of Father Abd el-Mesih, so he took a glass of water, and upon his entry he sprayed some of the water on him and made the sign of the cross on him. Father Abd el-Mesih calmed down suddenly and silently sat down at his feet for the rest of the gathering. When Father Abd el-Mesih wanted to leave, he pleaded with Pope Kyrollos to pray for him and asked his blessing, so he prayed for him and let him go.

When the number of visitors began to increase and disturb his peace, he left his cell and asked one of his dearly loved brothers to take him to the Papal residence in Egypt. When he got there, they told him that the Pope took refuge in a cell when he had had an exhausting day. However he complained in his usual way to those talking to him, and he went up to the residence of the Pope. When the Pope felt his presence, he came out and joyfully greeted him and listened to his complaint intently. He willingly agreed with Father Abd el-Mesih to notify the monastery to refuse any visitors coming to his cell, since he also knew how sweet and serene solitude is.

To calm him down, the Pope offered Father Abd el-Mesih some lupins (termes) - he only took three! Then he showed him that he had some Holy Bread, which was his food for the rest of the day. When it was inappropriate to go back to the desert as it was late, therefore he had to stay in the Papal residence, Father Abd el-Mesih refused the many pleas of the residents to offer him service. Instead of staying in the room they prepared especially for him, he slept on a pile of sand in the main grounds of the Papal residence. When Pope Kyrollos saw what had happened, he forbade any visitors from the monastery to visit Father Abd el-Mesih, saying, "Leave him, so that God may lift His wrath from the world for his sake."

Dr Nazeeh Asaad Younan says that every time he visited Father Abd el-Mesih, Father Abd el-Mesih would make him promise to deliver his greetings to Pope Kyrollos VI, and when he delivered the greetings, the Pope would reply saying, "What are we next to him?...He is one of the hermits."

His Relationship with Pope Shenouda III

The relationship between Pope Shenouda and Father Abd el-Mesih el-Habashi started when His Holiness was a novice monk looking for the ideal monastic life. When he found out about Father Abd el-Mesih, and saw in his life the ideal monastic life, he was greatly astonished at his asceticism and rejection of the world, and loved him greatly.

Father Abd el-Mesih also admired Father Antonious, and was pleased with his simplicity and his closeness to him. Father Abd el-Mesih also saw an asceticism in Father Antonious that he wished he could see all over Egypt. He was also pleased with his simple clothing and wooden stick.

The young monk Father Antonious was also delighted to know him. Father Abd el-Mesih's simplicity and poor outward appearance appealed to Father Antonious, which brought out in him the true meaning of monasticism that he was looking for.

Father Tawadrous el-Suriany recalls that when His Holiness the Pope (Father Antonious) had returned from St Samuel's Monastery, he sent news to Dr Wahib Attallah (Bishop Gregorious) that he was going to pass by Father Abd el-Mesih's cell on his way back. He stayed there for a few days before Father Macary el-Suriany (the Late Bishop Samuel) came to accompany him back to the monastery.

Father Antonious reached to the point where he wanted to live close to Father Abd el-Mesih, and he almost began digging a cave for himself, as Father Abd el-Mesih's had approved for him to do. However he could not continue as the Fathers in the Monastery convinced him to return. He then led the ascetic life by living in solitude close to the Surian Monastery, and lived there for some years.

Father Antonious (His Holiness the Pope) always sympathised with Father Abd el-Mesih, and cared for him, so much so that he even asked if he could make a door for Father Abd el-Mesih's cell, which he refused, leaving all his cares at the feet of the One for Whom he chose to live in the wilderness.

After Father Antonious received the grace of becoming a Bishop, he maintained a close relationship with Father Abd el-Mesih, visiting him from time to time. However he would ask his companions not to tell Father Abd el-Mesih that he had become a bishop, for he knew that this matter pained Father Abd el-Mesih. He always took care to make no signal or action that would lead to Father Abd el-Mesih finding out.

Father Yousab el-Suriany says that Father Abd el-Mesih prophesied His Holiness Pope Shenouda's ordination as Pope; this happened during one of his visits accompanied by the Late Father Theophilus.

Father Youssef el-Mahreky recalls one time when the Papal Seat was vacant, that some Protestant visitors came to Father Abd el-Mesih and asked him saying, "Pray that God will send a shepherd for His flock." So he cried and said, "When a foetus is born head first, it suffers no complications, but when it is born feet first, it causes death to the mother and to itself…" And as if he had just realised he was accompanied by visitors, he went on, saying, "What does it matter to you! You have deviated from the church!"

Very Reverend Father Anastasy el-Samuely also recalls that when the Altar's Lot chose His Holiness Pope Shenouda as Pope, he visited Father Abd el-Mesih along with Bishop Theophilus, Very Rev Father Sarabamoun el-Suriany (Bishop Sarabamoun of St Bishoy's Monastery), Very Rev Father Mattias el-Suriany (Bishop Reweis) and Very Rev Father Anastasy. His Holiness asked that no one tell Father Abd el-Mesih that he had been appointed by God as Pope, but miraculously, Father Abd el-Mesih started talking about the role of the leader towards his congregation, and the obligations of the Pope and the Bishop, and so on. In the end, Bishop Theophilus told him that His Holiness had been chosen as a Pope.

In the early days of the year 1972, that is, not more than a few months after His Holiness Pope Shenouda became Patriarch of the Holy See of St Mark, Father Abd el-Mesih el-Habashi left his cell, never to return there. He went to the Papal residence where he met His Holiness, who greeted him very joyfully and listened to his request. Father Abd el-Mesih requested that he be granted the Pope's blessing to travel to Jerusalem; he was granted absolution and permission to do so.

He intended to travel to Jerusalem on foot, as he had come from Ethiopia to Egypt on foot. However, the Pope feared that he might meet danger on the way, as the relationship between Israel and Egypt was quite tense at that time, so the Pope arranged a room for him to live in until he could prepare a proper way of getting him to Jerusalem safely.

Father Abd el-Mesih kept persisting and pleading with the Pope, as if he were a prisoner, until the Pope gave him permission to travel on a ship that would sail to Beirut, from which point he could enter Jerusalem. His Holiness wrote a lot about Father Abd el-Mesih in el Keraza Magazine, and published many of his pictures, as a sign of his unforgettable personality, and his great love toward him.

Pope Shenouda's Memories of the Ethiopian

When His Holiness was asked by some of the monks of St Mina's Monastery in Mariout about the life and ritual of Father Abd el-Mesih el-Habashi's monastic life, he replied saying, "I do not know a lot of details about his monastic life, for he did not speak unless he was interested in any subject matter. Even though I lived in the cell next door to his, I realised it was very hard for any monk to become his disciple. I distinctly remember asking him about some spiritual advice, and he replied saying, "Look, Father, I lived in Ethiopia a long time ago, then I left Ethiopia and started walking until I came to the Baramous Monastery." Then he continued to tell his life story of hardships he faced from the monastery, and his leaving the monastery to live in solitude in a cell. This story continued for about an hour. It started with his birth and ended with him living in solitude. When he finished his monologue, he looked at me and said, "I am not a monk or a priest and I don't know anything about what you say." Then he left me alone and went his way.

Despite this, we loved him sincerely, and would go to his cell carrying whatever we could of food and drink from the monastery. He was a very ascetic man indeed, and would fast all year long, not eating any meat or fish at all. We would carry him vegetables, oil, honey, and the like.

He would sit with us and tell us stories, but we never asked him any questions, because he would not answer. He had a very unique way of teaching, for once he drew on the ground what looked like a monastery and an ocean, and he said, "A monk is like a fish in the sea: if it leaves the sea, it dies instantly." He was also like that with his advice, as he would advise whoever needed advice without being asked to do so.

One of the signs of brotherly love between Father Abd el-Mesih and I was the fact that I used to help him speak Arabic, for he only knew how to speak Ethiopian. When he needed to know a specific word, he told me to read a Psalm in Arabic until I came to the word whose meaning he needed to know, and would point it out to me. He also used to change letters around because of his very limited knowledge of the Arabic language.

There were times when he could not get food from the Baramous Monastery, so he would walk from his cell to the Surian Monastery instead to get his food and drink. Due to the extended distance he had to walk, his body looked more and more frail, until one day he lost consciousness close to the Baramous Monastery. Some of the monks found him and took him inside the monastery and offered him food. When he finished eating he said, "Look, Father, I ate, I drank and I talked, and there are no more rules set by Saint Macarius that I have not broken yet." This was due to the fact that Saint Macarius set rules which prohibited a monk from eating, drinking or talking with laypeople.

Father Abd el-Mesih el-Habashi was a very simple man, but at the same time he was very courageous in what he said. For example, two Ethiopian bishops came to visit the monastery, so I took them to Father Abd el-Mesih when he was still dwelling in the monastery. When the bishops were about to leave, Father Abd el-Mesih clung to the clothes of one of the bishops and said in a sad tone, "What is this, my Father? Are you a Prime Minister?" He did not agree with their fancy way of dress, and he did not pay any respect to high authorities in general.

This happened again when Father Abd el-Mesih found out that there were bishops visiting the monastery, so he asked if he could meet with them to take their blessings. However, the monks who knew of Father Abd el-Mesih's great honesty dreaded that meeting, even though Father Abd el-Mesih promised he would not say anything to the bishops. So when the bishops arrived, and the monastery's bells rang, he heard them from his cell, which was about 30 minutes' walk from the monastery. So he came down and the monks took him to where the bishops were sitting. Looking into the room from a distance, he saw a bed, a desk and a comfortable chair. At that moment, he covered his eyes with his hands and cried out, "I can't do it, my Fathers...I can't do it...Leave me alone, Fathers, for this cell is not a monk's cell but a king's." The monks felt ashamed and left.

He would always eat dried food, which led to some health complications for Father Abd el-Mesih, including constipation. When his visitors found out about his deteriorating health, they advised him to go to Cairo for treatment. They asked him if he knew anybody from Cairo, to which he replied, "Pope Shenouda." So when he came to Cairo, came to the Papal residency, and knocked on my door, I greeted him, and took him straight to my study, which was full of books. I did not want him to see my bedroom, so that he would not criticize it's furniture - as he did with other bishops-and return to the monastery without treatment!

When he sat down and explained his illness to me, I got up and talked with a doctor on the phone to schedule an appointment. Father Abd el-Mesih was greatly surprised at the piece of metal I was talking into! When he asked, I told him it was a phone, but he replied, "No, this is a devil," and left my cell saying, "No more!" meaning that I should not use the phone any more. However I could not promise him that! Thus from that point onwards, whenever he saw me talking on the phone, he would repeat, "This is a devil, my Father."

I remember that when I took the cave near his, I found it immersed in sand, so I started cleaning it. When he saw me, he said, "No work today." I asked him why, and he said, "Today is the feast of the Archangel Michael," so I obeyed him and stopped working.

In his final days, he asked to visit Jerusalem, and he came to the Papal residence to ask my permission to do so. When I heard his request, I offered to arrange a plane flight for him, but he refused, saying that he would rather walk there. At that time, there was war between Egypt and Israel, so I refused his request, fearing for his life. Finally, I sent him with an Ethiopian son who was studying in the Theological College; he was to take him by ship to Jordan, and from there to Israel. However, from the time that I sent him off, we never heard any more from him.

I remember I wrote an article in el-Keraza magazine, titled *The great cave man went to Jerusalem."* This was wrongly understood by readers for his having gone to the heavenly Jerusalem (meaning that he had passed away). However it is most probable that he passed away in Jerusalem.

He was truly a man of solitude; he lived in solitude and asceticism and courage, away from the pleasures and joys of life. He walked barefoot; his cell did not even have a door.

I remember when Bishop Theophilus began renovating the monastery, for he was the first person to renovate in the desert - he built the first water tank in the entire desert. Father Abd el-Mesih came to visit the monastery, went inside the church and prostrated himself in front of each of the icons of the saints. This was his way of taking their blessing. When he had finished, he sat down with Bishop Theophilus, who started telling him of his many plans for the monastery. When he finished talking, expecting encouragement or words of praise, Father Abd el-Mesih simply said, 'Martha, Martha, you work a lot!'" At this point, Bishop Theophilus was filled with shame and embarrassment. Father Abd el-Mesih did not know how to give compliments, but he would tell the truth to whomever he was speaking to.

FOUR

WAY OF LIFE AND TEACHINGS

FATHER ABD EL-MESIH EL-HABASHI did not act out of ignorance or insanity. However, he had a spiritual and ascetic attitude, which reflected on his actions, so that all his actions were a reflection of what was going on inside his heart.

He left his very wealthy family - he even left his country - and chose to live with no name, and when the monks asked him, the reason for leaving the world and becoming a monk; he said, "Goodness was overflowing, but there was no Christ." This was the same reason he repeated if people showed him sympathy for the hardships he faced because of a lack of proper food and rest, or the dangers of travelling on foot.

Thus, he used to look for God wherever he went, and in whatever way possible, with his poor body but enlightened heart he would repeat, "Lord, I will follow You wherever You go." (Luke 9:57) He realised that the materialistic world would not satisfy him, but that it was more acceptable to sell all his possessions to win his eternity.

This was the same, simple idea that encouraged the great pillars of monasticism to reject the world, along with everyone and everything in it, placing their hope in God, who never forsook them. For they ridiculed the world and its pleasures, looking down on its vainglory and repeating with Saint Paul saying, "For we brought nothing into this world, and it is certain we can carry nothing out." (1 Timothy 6:7)

Everyone who talked with Father Abd el-Mesih bore witness to his extensive knowledge of the Holy Bible, and how he memorised most of it by heart, and how he would explain any questions asked by others with great clarity.

On top of all that, he was an expert in the sayings of the desert Fathers, especially the ascetical homilies of St Isaac the Syrian. This was clear from his teachings, and from how greatly enlightened by Saint Isaac the Syrian's sayings he was. He found refuge in stories of the saints, which he knew and followed day by day.

Once he was deeply troubled by annoying thoughts, and it happened that one of his visitors was Father Armeya el-Baramousy, who sat down with him and told him the story of the martyrdom of Saint Victor of Egypt. Father Abd el-Mesih was overjoyed in spirit and found immense consolation in this saint's pure life. It is most probable that he realised how merciful God was to appear to a holy young man like Saint Victor.

Saint Isaac the Syrian says, "Every time a man

rejects this world, and heed in his heart the fear of God, the more he will feels His care and His strength mysteriously in him, and springs from him pure thoughts. Inasmuch as he keeps himself from the pleasures of the world, God's mercy will follow him, and he will be overwhelmed by God's love for mankind."

Father Abd el-Mesih el-Habashi was wise in his asceticism, for he would eat food that would help him to live to the age of 80. He was not very strict, acting without understanding, but he knew exactly how too much food brings war upon a man, distracts his thoughts and darkens his understanding. He told Meinardus, replying to the many failed attempts of monks to get him to eat proper food, "They should know that whoever pleases himself by eating fish and oil (he meant sardines), has Satan come by night and become his master."

Father Theophilus el-Baramousy says that Father Abd el-Mesih el-Habashi always connected a monk's true love for Christ with no indulgences or bodily comforts. He would say that a true monk does not care about food or clothing.

His only wish was for all monks to lead the same life he led himself. What is amazing is that despite his great asceticism, he often talked of Mani's Heresy, pulling it apart with great knowledge and specific understanding, both spiritual and ascetic.

When others would warn him about his extreme asceticism, he would reply confidently and joyously saying, "If I am sick, my physician is Jesus, who will take better care of me." This meant that his asceticism was not a competition or a race to win the vainglory or praise of others.

His Balanced and Flexible Life

He spent 36 years in the desert in his cave. He had a routine of receiving gifts from visitors, and then giving them to other visitors. We know that there are two main forms of asceticism, which should be followed: Firstly, freedom from all worldly possessions, according to Saint Moses the Black, who said, "Love of possessions deters the mind, but asceticism enlightens it." The second: Not clinging to any worldly possessions, about which a hermit Father said, "Owning possessions does not bring us harm, but it is our sorrow at losing them that harms us."

He forced himself to follow a plan, and would remain consistent in the amount of food he allowed himself, and in how he ate his food.

Amazingly, he was not blindly tough on himself, holding back on what he truly needed. On the contrary, despite his great asceticism, he would leave his cell many times to visit Wadi el-Natroun, Cairo or Alexandria. However, he would spend his nights away from his cell performing the same ritual he was accustomed to back in the desert. This would allow him to return to his cell as if he had never left it in the first place! This implied that his heart was with God, regardless of his physical existence. Tamav (Mother) Sarah commented about this phenomenon saying, "A man might be alone by himself, but his thoughts are deeply busied with affairs of others."

Even though he was tough with himself, Father Abd el-Mesih was gentle with others. He was a rare breed of ascetic, but at the same time, he welcomed visitors generously. He loved solitude and quietness, but would joyfully receive any strangers with a warm smile.

Father Anastasy el-Samuely says, "Father Abd el-Mesih el-Habashi used to think that a monk who works more, eats more and conversely, a monk who works less, eats less. Thus, his characteristics and virtues were never a product of routine, which he might have claimed from some Ethiopian or Egyptian monks, for a virtue is a spiritual work. Virtue has deep roots in the innermost parts of a man, whereas routine has a shallow effect. Routine is only a crust which results from mental strife, but does not produce fruits of the Spirit."

His Courage

Father Abd el-Mesih el-Habashi's true inner strength may have stemmed from his indifferent nature toward everything. His fearless attitude was even more mysterious. This is reflected in Saint Augustine's saying, "I felt like I was on top of the world, when I ceased fearing anything, or desiring anything."

Father Abd el-Mesih knew that the whole universe was God's perfect creation. Every living thing in it belonged to Him. Accordingly, he was never afraid of wild animals. His cell had no door, and sometimes it became infested with scorpions and many serpents.

Many monks who visited Father Abd el-Mesih witness that there was a serpent which came and coiled itself on his lap. Father Abd el-Mesih would just sit, motionless and quiet.

Bishop Isozorous (Abbot of the Baramous Monastery) recounts that once, while Father Abd el-Mesih was standing and praying with two other bishops, a serpent slithered close to them, with a loud hissing noise. The bishops were somewhat alarmed, but Father Abd el-Mesih was all the more calm.

He even tamed wolves around him, so he did not fear them, nor did they fear him. Mr Ragheb Moftah says that once he spent a long time with Father Abd el-Mesih in his cell, until it was very late, so he was forced to go back to the monastery in the dark. So Father Abd el-Mesih prayed and pointed him in the direction of the monastery, and said, "Do not fear those things that look like dogs if they show up." (Meaning the wolves)

Some of the servants who visited Father Abd el-Mesih said that when they brought him some guava, they realised that they should have thrown away the ones that had gone bad. But Father Abd el-Mesih warned them gently, saying, "Leave them here (pointing to a corner of the cell), so that the serpent can find something to eat!!" Others said that they saw a scorpion close to Father Abd el-Mesih, so one of them hurried to go kill it, but Father Abd el-Mesih warned him saying, "There is more of that inside!"

The well known journalist Mr Raafat Botrous recounts a story that happened to Father Abd el-Mesih: He said that a huge serpent quickly slithered straight toward Father Abd el-Mesih and bit him, not to kill him, but to prevent his certain death caused by eating some poisonous grass in the desert. The venom of this serpent worked as an antidote against the poisonous grass, and so Father Abd el-Mesih lived.

Rizk Iskander says that he once asked Father Abd el-Mesih whether he saw wolves out in the desert. Father Abd el-Mesih replied saying that he had seen a wolf a few days before, coming and standing right in front of him, carrying a duck in its mouth! So he made the sign of the cross over the wolf, and it left him quietly.

Rev Father Mikhail Saad comments saying, "Father

Abd el-Mesih has become comfortable with beasts, so that he does not fear them, and neither do they fear him." He himself told Father Armeya el-Baramousy that in the first period that Father Abd el-Mesih spent in his new cell, a huge serpent came out, but Father Abd el-Mesih blew air in its face. Father Armeya wondered how it was that the serpent did not harm him, to which Father Abd el-Mesih replied saying, "You do not know God!"

Father Sawires says that Father Abd el-Mesih used to say, "God has given us authority over creatures, not so we can kill them, but only so we can escape harm." One of the workers of Father Sawires once saw a hyena in front of Father Abd el-Mesih's cave. Father Tadrous el-Baramousy says he saw him carry a scorpion in his hands with gentleness and without fear, in order to take it out of his cave. Father Bemin el-Suriany says he saw Father Abd el-Mesih and a snake eating from the same plate!

What is comical about this is that when people started showing pity towards him because of his poor and extremely ascetic life, and asked him, "Do you not fear that a wolf might attack you?" he would reply saying, "Would a wolf attack another wolf?!!"

His Courage in Discipline

No doubt there is a difference between courage and insanity, for a courageous person has a strong personality, and is filled with victory and self control, which aids his strength in disciplining and chastising others. No man can be strong and courageous unless he truly is victorious over his weaknesses and pains, otherwise what he calls courage is actually pride and self-centredness. This is why our Lord Christ revealed

His courage in one sentence, "Which of you convicts Me of sin?" (John 8:46)

Those people who were disciplined by Father Abd el-Mesih el-Habashi accepted it with joy and deep affection.

If he talks about asceticism, he is a great ascetic.

If he talks about humility, he is very humble.

If he talks about spiritual struggles, he is a struggler of unique characteristics.

Overall, whatever virtue he spoke of, he was a perfect example of that virtue, "For out of the abundance of the heart his mouth speaks." (Luke 6:45)

Many Fathers agreed on the one saying that Father Abd el-Mesih was the modern day saint. Father Philoxinous el-Suriany says he is like Elijah the prophet in his strength and courage. Bishop Isaac says he is like John the Baptist in his zealous heart and courage, as well as his ascetic way of life. Regarding his courage, Father Anastasy el-Samuely also says, "He did not fear people, nor beasts, nor devils. Father Abd el-Mesih was a symbol of God's power in man."

Whenever Father Abd el-Mesih heard about a monk accepting the rank of Bishop, he would rebuke him and criticise him bitterly for leaving his monastic life to live in a world that could take him away from God. When he heard about the ordination of an Ethiopian bishop, he was saddened and pained by it. His reason was that bishops in Ethiopia should be Egyptians, because the one who delivered the Coptic faith to Ethiopia was an Egyptian.

Bishop Macarius the Ethiopian recalls an occasion when he decided to return to the world to study in the Theological College in Mahmasha, Cairo, and Father Abd el-Mesih found out about it. He asked Bishop Macarius, "Does this mean you will not practise the rites of our Fathers Saint Anthony and Saint Macarius?" He replied, "No," then added in a humble but laughing tone, "Even in the monastery there are no rites of Saint Anthony and Saint Macarius." However Father Abd el-Mesih took this very seriously, and was deeply sorrowful because he thought it meant that there are no rites of Saint Anthony and Saint Macarius in any of the monasteries.

He was strongly against monks wearing soft clothing, repeating what our Lord Christ said about Saint John the Baptist, saying, "Those who wear soft clothing are in kings' houses." (Matthew 11:8) Father Yousab el-Suriany says that once a monk asked Father Abd el-Mesih if he could stay with him in his cell, not because he wanted to, but for the prestige. Father Abd el-Mesih looked at him sternly and said in a strict tone, "Your heart is deviant!"

He himself once told two elderly monks from the monastery (Very Rev Fathers Tadrous and Mansour) that if it were up to him to lead the monastery as abbot, he would have limited all the supplies used by the monks, such as food and water. He would even have sealed off the water tank, saying that a monk should live on one bottle of water a day!

One of the elderly desert Fathers, who refused to give his name, said that Father Abd el-Mesih used to remind him of Saint John the Baptist, and he recalls this amazing story: "In the early fifties, I was in a group of youth going for a retreat to the monastery. We were standing outside the door, until Father Abd el-Mesih came from his cell. Some of the monks from the monastery came out to greet Father Abd el-Mesih, and one of them starting joking with him saying, "Emperor Haile Selassie has given an order for Father Abd el-Mesih to be ordained as a Bishop." To respond to such ill-conceived joke, Father Abd el-Mesih sternly glared at the monk with penetrating eyes and rebuked him saying, "Is there no door to the bathroom!" This meant that such inappropriate talk only came from inappropriate places.

Despite this incident, when he was visiting the Surian Monastery, he met some of the Fathers and rebuked them because they were not living the true monastic life. He was forced to stay the night, so he slept inside the entrance of the monastery, outside the church. That night was one of the nights of the Kiahk Praises, where monks stay up all night praising and praying until sunrise. When he met those monks again in the morning, he apologised to them for rebuking them the previous day, saying, "Good monks...good monks."

Bishop Macarius the Ethiopian also recalls a time when two Ethiopian bishops wanted to visit Father Abd el-Mesih. They brought a bus driver called Ismael along with them so that they could easily find the way to his cell. When they arrived at his cell, they called out to him to come out and meet them, but when Father Abd el-Mesih laid eyes on the bishops' fancy clothes, he sat on the ground far away from them and would not get up and greet them. After a long period of time, Father Abd el-Mesih finally spoke, saying, "Devils... Devils...why have you not cared about your duty of care to your congregations instead of this enjoyable life?" He then got up, entered his cell, and would not come out. With that, the bishops retreated and returned to Cairo.

It is important to note that his rebuke of others is not a translation of any anger he had in his heart towards them, nor did it cause him to lose his peace. If a monk cannot control his short temper, he will not last a single day in solitude, unlike Father Abd el-Mesih, who lasted many years. These shortcomings are traced back to the love inside his heart toward others.

We should not forget that sometimes when Father Abd el-Mesih would say words that had heavy underlying meanings, he would choose them out of his ignorance, simply because he was not Egyptian like his visitors. Even though he lived in Egypt for 40 years, he was never fluent in the Arabic language up until the time of his departure; he therefore knew little about what he said as words of rebuke. In return, whenever anyone accused him of any wrongdoing, he would smile like a child and would never return any hatred from others, which would indicate that his rebuke was out of love and not anger.

Father Yousef el-Mahreky says that Father Abd el-Mesih never got angry; even if someone insulted him, he would smile and quickly kiss the hand of the one who insulted him, saying, "I have sinned; forgive me, my Father," but of course in his own accent.

Father Armeya el-Baramousy said that Father Abd el-Mesih's heart was very tender towards everyone, without exception. Once when he was visiting Father Abd el-Mesih, he wanted to walk around the cave for a while, but Father Abd el-Mesih refused, worrying about his safety because of creeping things or wild beasts.

Here is a story which highlights Father Abd el-Mesih's acceptance to insults with joy and a childlike demeanour. Mr Rizk Iskander recalls an incident when he met Father Abd el-Mesih outside the monastery door, in the presence of Father Yacoub el-Baramousy. Father Abd el-Mesih sat on the ground and started weaving palm leaves to make a basket, which he had already started making on his way from his cell to the monastery. Father Yacoub then said out loud, "Did you know that Father Abd el-Mesih is a very holy saint, and no one pays attention to him..?" Father Abd el-Mesih sat silently, pretending not to be listening, and thus Father Yacoub kept commending him, but to no avail: Father Abd el-Mesih would not turn around, but kept working silently on his basket. As a change of tactics, Father Yacoub then said aloud, "Did you also know that Father Abd el-Mesih is a donkey?" At this point, Father Abd el-Mesih laughed and was joyful, and exclaimed, "Correct...correct...I am a donkey!"

The same thing occurred again when Father Marcos El Sabky was in the presence of Father Youssef el-Baramousy and Father Abd el-Mesih. They were talking for a while, when finally Father Marcos asked Father Abd el-Mesih to pray for him, but Father Yousef interrupted them and told Father Marcos that Father Abd el-Mesih could not pray for him because he was incapable, he was a donkey! Father Abd el-Mesih was delighted and cheerfully agreed, saying, "True, true, I am a donkey." Father Yousef only said this to show his visitors how humble Father Abd el-Mesih was, not to tease him.

Other Fathers and even servants concur that Father Abd el-Mesih was truly humble. Many saw workers in the Anba Reweis papal residence abuse and insult him. His only response was silence, calmness and peace.

His Relationship with the Church

Not one monk from his monastery saw Father Abd el-Mesih enter the church, except on Maundy Thursday, to gain the blessings of the washing of the feet with the water of the Lakan. However, to understand Father

Abd el-Mesih's respect for the Holy Sacraments of the church, let us consider this story:

Bishop Isaac recalls, "When Father Abd el-Mesih was on his way to meet the late Pope Kyrollos, he passed by the Surian Monastery. It was time for the Sunset Prayer, so he entered the church and prostrated himself before each icon, taking dust from under each and putting it on his head and clothes. He then rose and went straight to the abbot of the monastery and begged earnestly for him to pray the three absolution prayers, so he did." In Cairo, when he was getting ready to travel to Jerusalem, he asked if he could visit the places that the Holy Family visited, so they took him to those places. He repeated the same action in each church he entered.

However, the reason behind him not attending Holy Communion every week is a mystery. There is some speculation over the reason. Bishop Isaac says that Ethiopian monks have a misconception that partaking of the Holy Communion is for children under the age of six, and elderly people over sixty. This is due to their belief that Communion is only for the worthy, because those under the age of six are still pure, and those over the age of sixty are better prepared for their eternity because of their repentance and good deeds!

Bishop Isaac continues, "When the late Pope Kyrollos visited Ethiopia and found out about this misunderstanding, he corrected it and convinced them that Communion is essential throughout the life of each person. Nevertheless, Father Abd el-Mesih was well beyond the age of sixty when he left his Monastery, since he was born in 1898 and left the Monastery in 1971, yet as far as all the monks witnessed, he never partook of the Eucharist. Did he partake of the Holy Communion in another place? Did he reach the level of the hermits?

We cannot conclude this with certainty, even though many think so, because it is virtually impossible for such a monk to reach this incredible level of virtue without a constant relationship with the Holy Eucharist. The Sacrament of the Eucharist unites him with Christ, and gives him characteristics and virtues, because every time he has Communion, he proclaims Christ's death, and His resurrection.

The Fathers of the Baramous monastery confirms this idea, since they asked him where he had Communion and he would always avoid answering their question. However, no one is sure where he had Communion.

Very Rev Father Antonious Younan recalls the time when he was amongst other people, and they were discussing how Father Abd el-Mesih used to have Communion, so they asked the abbot of the Monastery, the Very Rev Father Dawood el-Baramousy, but he tried to change the subject. They forced him to return to the topic and kept nagging him until he confirmed that Father Abd el-Mesih did partake of the Holy Communion, but he would not reveal any more information. However, Father Yousef el-Mahrcky, who was closest to Father Abd el-Mesih, agreed that Father Abd el-Mesih partook in Communion on feasts.

Father Markos el-Sabky said that he visited Father Abd el-Mesih with Father Yousef el-Baramousy, because he had previously asked them if he could borrow a clamp to pull out a tooth that was irritating him and causing him pain. They gave it to him, and asked him to use it then and there so that they could take it back to the monastery with them, but he refused, saying that he could not use it on that particular day. They understood that he had had Communion, but where?

On many occasions, Father Abd el-Mesih was seen exiting St Mark's Church in Alexandria. This was during the time when he was seeing a doctor in Alexandria and he was also receiving the blessing of the body of St Mark. Father Michael Saad and Mr Nabil Naeem Tadros were witnesses to these events.

Did He Reach the Level of Hermits?

We cannot confirm whether he reached the level of a hermit, but many Fathers agree that it could be true. Very Rev Father Anastasy el-Samuely says that he asked one of the Ethiopian bishops if he knew of any Ethiopian hermits, and to his surprise the answer was that there was a whole monastery for hermits! This was why Father Anastasy thought that Father Abd el-Mesih had reached the level of hermit, and could partake of Holy Communion and attend the liturgy with other hermits on that basis.

Very Rev Father Mansour el-Baramousy said that he is not surprised that Father Abd el-Mesih partook of the Holy Communion. Father Mina el-Baramousy says that there would be no chance that such a person could excel in his spiritual level had he not partaken of the Holy Sacraments. Hence it is essential and certain that Father Abd el-Mesih would have partaken of the Holy Communion with hermits.

Mr George Tesfay, an employee in the Ethiopian Embassy, revealed that he heard Father Philemon el-Mahreky say that he was present when Father Abd el-Mesih stayed at the monastery, and that he knew Father Abd el-Mesih had reached the level of hermit.

Father Yousef el-Mahreky set our guessing straight with words from the mouth of Father Abd el-Mesih.

He once asked him if he partook of Holy Communion, and Father Abd el-Mesih replied saying, "Did Saint Paula, the first of hermits, have Holy Communion?" He answered, "Of course." So Father Abd el-Mesih continued, "And I, too, have Holy Communion on such a basis," and smiled with his simple nature.

His Stance on the Ethiopian Church

As an Ethiopian citizen and monk, Father Abd el-Mesih el-Habashi had a wealth of knowledge of the rites of the Church and the rites belonging to the ordination of bishops, and he clearly knew that St Matthew introduced the Coptic Faith to Ethiopia. He knew that the first ordained bishop of Ethiopia was Bishop Salama, who was ordained by Pope Athanasius the Apostolic in the year 330 AD. Since then, all the Ethiopian bishops had been Coptic monks.

When Father Abd el-Mesih left Ethiopia for Scetis, he was under the ordinance of Bishop Kyrollos, who had been ordained as Bishop on the 2nd of June 1929. He left for Scetis in 1934, however he was surprised to hear that in the year 1951, an Ethiopian monk was ordained as a Metropolitan, and was given the authority to ordain other bishops - this was Metropolitan Bacillius. This marked the first Ethiopian monk in Ethiopian history to be ordained as bishop of Ethiopia.

Father Abd el-Mesih el-Habashi was deeply angered and much provoked, because he considered this as deviating from the rites of the early church fathers. He saw as this move away from the Mother Church and towards independence as one fuelled by self-pride, which had spread amongst the young Ethiopian laypeople. When he saw some of the Ethiopian monks visiting him, he would rebuke them and say, "You have destroyed it!" (Meaning Ethiopia)

It is essential to add that one hundred and nine metropolitans were ordained over Ethiopia, all of whom are Coptic monks.

In 1959, in the days of Pope Kyrollos the Sixth, Egypt and Ethiopia signed an agreement to raise the level of the archbishop of Eritrea to the equivalent of a patriarch.

After this news spread, Mr Mosaad Sadek (a journalist) met with Father Abd el-Mesih in his cell, where he found him deeply upset and pained over this agreement; he considered it a bad sign, and said that this agreement would cause many troubles and possibly catastrophes for Ethiopia and for Emperor Haile Selassie.

Mr Mosaad Sadek then proceeded to write an article in which he mentioned that Father Abd el-Mesih did not hesitate to rebuke close relatives of the Emperor, and when they visited him in his cell, he bitterly blamed them for making such an agreement, trying to rebel against the Mother Church. He warned them that the first people affected by such an agreement would be the Emperor's family. His visitors marvelled at Father Abd el-Mesih's courage in his stance. Mr Sadek highlighted the fact that in mid April 1980, Father Abd el-Mesih received a message from Ethiopia saying that the famine caused by the drought in Ethiopia has stretched its unmerciful hands to *Wello*, the birthplace of Father Abd el-Mesih el-Habashi.

His Teachings

Just as father Abd el-Mesih el-Habashi left the world to join the monastery, he left the monastery to live in a cave in the mountain, but he was still a living member of the church. We are many members of the one Body, a complete, unshakeable unity, for a monk works everywhere. If the world is an assembly of individuals, it is not overcrowded, but a unified body.

His Interaction with the Church Fathers

When monks came knocking on his door, he would never turn them away or deprive them of his time or experience, for he would talk to them about asceticism and how to control one's thoughts. If he ever wanted to describe a monk not living up to the required standard, he would say, "A broken monk", which means that his relationship with Christ is not the correct one.

When one of the monks would return from the world, after working there for the sake of the monastery, he would ask him about how Christians in the world were living, and about the level of persecution – much like Saint Paula used to ask Saint Anthony, and bishop Morkos used to ask bishop Pafnotius. He would ask about whether Christians fasted, and whether they still performed miracles like their forefathers.

If he found out that people were indulging in their lives, gathering the fruits of the earth and cutting down on their relationship with the church, he would become very upset and pained. If he heard that the devil was attacking the leaders, he would become very edgy, and would start repeating his famous words, "It is all broken...all broken."

When he became upset about the news of the Christians of the world, his feelings were genuine! This was the true and direct effect of his deep love toward the church, and his great struggles supported such emotions. He did not fear the criticism of others, because he was not broken!

Bishop Isaac said that whenever he visited Father Abd el-Mesih with some fellow monks, they would get a good pounding from him, but they truly loved him for it, because he rebuked them in the spirit of love, and he rebuked not only them, but all monks in general.

Father Yousef el-Mahreky said once that one of the abbots of one of the monasteries of Egypt – probably bishop Theophillus, abbot of the Surian Monastery – visited Father Abd el-Mesih and asked him saying, "When will monasticism return to its original glory?" Father Abd el-Mesih answered saying, "It will return to its original glory when all gold and silver is as fuel, thrown into the fire to be burnt (meaning that it becomes of no value)." He continued and incorporated the saying of Father Bakhomious, Father of Community, saying, "It is not right that a monk should own money, silver or gold."

Father Philoxinus el-Suriany says that even though Father Abd el-Mesih started out without a mentor, he would always advise new monks to seek advice, and would personally share his experience with them. This was like a child trying to cross a river; he would need a person to teach him how to swim in order to be able to cross the river.

In addition, in a very rare voice recording of Father Abd el-Mesih, he advised his beloved to each have a teacher to teach them all things. He added that a monk in the beginning of monasticism needs spiritual milk, as a baby needs its mother's milk. This type of advice was mainly directed towards youth intending to walk the path of monasticism.

Most of the priests who visited him in his cell to ask him for spiritual guidance on the responsibilities of a priest were the priests who spent their 40 days in the monastery after ordination. Among these priests were Father Mikhaiel Saad, Botros Guirguis and many others. They used to come by his cell, hear his advice and ask him for guidance.

Father Bishoy Kamel wrote in his memoirs that during his 40 days that followed his ordination, he visited Father Abd el-Mesih and they talked about service, and the responsibilities and duties of a priest.

With His Lay Visitors

He was more tolerant with his lay visitors, possibly because he acknowledged that the mistakes of the congregation were out of negligence, whereas the mistakes of the priests were sins.

Whenever he used to see a layperson from afar coming to visit him, he would quickly go into his cell and stay there a little while before coming out to greet his visitor: He used to pray in every instance before talking to others.

Father Mikhaiel Saad recalls when he first visited Father Abd el-Mesih el-Habashi in 1957: "We were with a group of monks, and when we were about 500 metres away, we saw him standing on top of his cell, like a dry stick. When he spotted us, he quickly went into his cell. We continued to walk until we came to his cell, but the monk who was our tour guide told us to sit down quietly, until Father Abd el-Mesih came out of his own accord. We sat down and talked quietly amongst ourselves for about 15 minutes until Father Abd el-Mesih appeared from his cell. He was like John the Baptist; he was very skinny, dark skinned, with dirty clothes, and bare feet. We tried to kiss his hand but he would not allow us to. We finally sat at a sand dune, and he sat atop it.

"His poor Arabic language was a barrier to his self-expression. He talked about matters pertaining to the church, and others pertaining to the world, all of which were aimed at the profanity of the world that had entered the church, and the people of high status who live in the pride of life. After saying any of this, he would pause and let out a groan of pain from inside him towards these people. His pained groans were mixed with bitter sorrow, apparent from the way he used to bow his head, rub his forehead and groan silently."

In the rare voice recording, it was very apparent how little Arabic Father Abd el-Mesih knew and used. In the half hour of recording, you could easily count the few words he spoke. He mainly spoke Tigrinya (his original language), so his visitors helped him express what he meant in Arabic.

He knew most, if not all, of the Holy Bible in his language, and if he ever needed to recite a verse, he would quickly run through it and stop at the verse he wanted to use to explain to his visitors. Of course, he would not be able to say it in perfect Arabic. In addition, Father Yousab el-Suriany says that once Father Abd el-Mesih wanted to talk about the pompous and arrogant leaders, he mentioned the verse spoken by Christ saying: "Woe to you, scribes and Pharisees, hypocrites! For you shut up the kingdom of heaven against men; for you neither go in yourselves, nor do you allow those who are entering to go in." (Matthew 23:13) But instead, he said, "You don't enter; you don't let them enter either!"

Father Mikhaiel Saad comments saying, "If this man knew Arabic well, he would have given us a great insight of the zealous heart he had, full of the Holy Spirit. To our great sorrow, his words expressed only a tiny fraction of what dwelled in his heart."

Dr Nazeeh Asaad says that when he would have the blessing of visiting Father Abd el-Mesih in the company of other visitors, their hearts would fill with spiritual joy and gladness when they were with him, when he talked to them using verses from the Bible in his Tigrinya language, trying to translate them into Arabic. He usually failed to do so correctly, but he used to repeat the Proverbs with great insights and the virtues of good character.

Saad Mattias says that when he would visit Father Abd el-Mesih with other visitors, Father Abd el-Mesih would discern what was inside each of their hearts without them mentioning it to him. They would go back home filled with comfort and joy from the Holy Spirit.

Saad Mattias says that Father Abd el-Mesih would recite long portions of the Holy Gospel in his Tigrinya language until he came to the verse he wished to discuss or mention to them.

Mr Fayek Fares says that he visited Father Abd el-Mesih in the Papal residence, and when he was still outside, he looked up and saw a big dove flying out of Father Abd el-Mesih's room, then his door opened and he came out. Mr Fares was still mesmerised by what he saw, so Father Abd el-Mesih approached him and pointed up and said, "The Paraclete...The Holy Spirit deciphers what is written!"

This actually meant that the Holy Spirit aided Father Abd el-Mesih in understanding what he could not perceive in the Holy Bible. *The Paradise of the Desert Fathers* mentions this matter, where a monk prays for Moses the Prophet, for example, to help him understand anything vague in the Torah books (the books of the Law).

Examples Used in His Teachings

As previously mentioned, Father Abd el-Mesih el-Habashi lacked fluency in the Arabic language. Many elderly Fathers in the past either did not want to reveal their spiritual experiences and connections, or lacked the means to describe them in words. Those able to express their experiences, and to pass them down to their spiritual children, were few. Most of the desert stories collated into books and the like, were passed down from past generations to us, through people who took great care to collect these sayings – as Palladius did, for example.

The Egyptian desert fathers in general used teach from past experience to a great extent in their lives. They used stories of older desert fathers to explain something to other people, and this of course is the life experience of highly spiritual individuals. These elderly saints learnt from our Lord Christ, as is written, "Without a parable He did not speak to them." (Matthew 13:34)

The Beginning of a Monk

When asked about caring for a novice monk, Father Abd el-Mesih told Father Philoxinus that a monk needs a teacher, just as a person who wants to learn how to swim is taken to the sea by his teacher, who trains him slowly but steadily. He stays close by, so that if he starts to drown, the teacher can quickly come to his rescue. In teaching him, the teacher swims by his side, so that the student can copy his teacher in his style. Therefore when he is ready, his teacher can let him swim by himself, and his only need for his teacher would be in special cases.

In another example to a novice monk, Father Abd el-Mesih said that he is like a baby being nursed by his mother. His mother nurses him for months on end, never letting him go. The baby cannot survive without his mother, because he cannot supply his own food by himself. The mother nurses her baby with love, and the baby does not leave his mother.

However, if he wanted to describe the difference between a monk who struggles, and another who does not struggle, he would place a small stone on top of another small stone on the ground. If the top stone stayed on top of the stone underneath, he would say happily, "This is a good monk." If, however, the stone fell down, he would say, "This monk is not good."

Father Bemin el-Suriany recalls that once, Father Abd el-Mesih wanted to describe what a monk's relationship with God should be like, so he wiped the ground with his hand, drew a large circle in the sand, and placed a large stone in its middle, pointed to it and said, "This is a city and the rock is the palace of the King. The monk is a resident of this city. If the monk is honest and trustworthy, the king honours him and allows him to live in His palace. If the monk breaks the law or rebels, the King will judge him and cast him out."

Father Yousab el-Suriany says that Father Abd el-Mesih once told him that a monk is like a soldier, whom the King sends to war in any condition, without food, drink or place to sleep. A true soldier would not care about any of that, and so does "a good monk," but if the monk rebels and flees from war, then "this monk is not good." This is how Father Abd el-Mesih would speak about the hard life that he lived when people asked, pitying him.

Bishop Macarius of Ethiopia says that Father Abd

el-Mesih is this very soldier, for his is the example of the courageous and honest soldier who does not choose particular wars, but listens to his King, and thus the King loves him very much.

Father Bemin el-Suriany recalls that Father Abd el-Mesih once told him, "A monk is like a lion in the desert. He is the king of the desert. If he deteriorates, the other beasts (the devils) mock him and attack him, and he loses his dignity."

Mr Rizk Iskander says that he was visiting Father Abd el-Mesih in the company of others, and when they decided to leave, one of them asked Father Abd el-Mesih to pray for him. He marvelled saying, "If the ship in the sea is in good condition and prepared, it will reach the other shore safely, but if it is not, then it will sink and will not reach the other shore." He presumably meant that prayer alone is not enough, but struggle and preparation on the part of the person are also needed.

Very Rev Father Antonious Younan says that he was visiting the monastery in 1943 and he met Father Abd el-Mesih at the door, so he indicated that his guests should sit down on the sand with him. He sat with them in front of a rock used for crushing wheat (a millstone). He put one stone on the rock, and another on the sand, to try to illustrate to them the meaning of the man who built his house on the rock, and the other who built his on the sand.

FIVE

LEAVING HIS CELL

One of the fathers who lived in solitude said that Father Abd el-Mesih el-Habashi used to leave his cave and walk in the desert for days on end. This happened many times.

The First Time

The first time he left his cell was presumably in the early 1950s, when he fell very ill, and was taken to a doctor due to the lack of proper medication available to save him. A man called Erian Iskander took him to the doctor, who became very worried, for upon routine checkups, he found that Father Abd el-Mesih el-Habashi's stomach had shrunk to the size of a three year old's. The doctor advised him to eat lots of food to recover, but Father Abd el-Mesih left the food in Mr Iskander's car. When he was forced to sleep overnight somewhere on his journey back to the monastery, he would not agree to sleep at Mr Iskander's house, but asked to be dropped off at the Papal residence to sleep there.

At the Papal residence, Father Abd el-Mesih el-Habashi met Very Rev Father Mikhaiel Saad, who said about his meeting, "He was on his way to mass, and I contemplated his appearance; indeed he had not changed one bit since I saw him at his cave, except for the fact that he was wearing very thin shoes, made of leather."

Father Abd el-Mesih also met a youth servant from Alexandria, Mr Nabil Naeem and he says about the meeting, "When we knew he was at the Papal residence, we went to him, and found him in the residency for visiting priests. We saw one of the Fathers pointing to the bed where he would be sleeping for the night. However, Father Abd el-Mesih disagreed about sleeping on a bed. He signalled that it was inappropriate for a monk to sleep like that, and he pointed at a place under the stairwell, wanting to sleep there for the night." Mr Naeem continues, saying, "This behaviour totally puts people who care excessively about the softness of their beds to shame."

He adds, "When we went to take his blessing the next day, he was coming out of church. A woman came to take his blessing, but her clothes may have been immodest, so when she came forward to kiss his hand, he said, "The world is turning into Sodom and Gomorrah; maybe fire will come down and consume it." He then said, "I am in a hurry," and he left."

His Meeting with the Holy Father Yustus el-Antony

Many fathers recall this wonderful incident:

Father Abd el-Mesih el-Habashi left his cell and start walking towards the Eastern Desert, until he came close to the monastery of Saint Anthony. A few metres before he reached the door, he started prostrating himself many times.

The monks inside the monastery were surprised to see Father Yustus also prostrating himself many times on his way to the door, and repeating, "Open the door... open the door." They thought that this was a symbolic gesture of their respect for one another, but it was as if each of them knew by the spirit that they would meet each other, and they went out to meet each other as Saint Anthony met Saint Paul in the desert. The Fathers of the monastery say that Father Yustus and Father Abd el-Mesih has longed to talk to each other.

Visiting the Monasteries in Upper Egypt

He did this in the 1950s, in October 1959 to be exact. He may have gone there to take blessing from the origins of the Coptic monasticism, in the Scetis Desert. Some people presumed that he was looking for a better place to live in as a monk, particularly the monasteries of Saint Pachomius. He had been much enlightened by the progress of Saint Pachomius in monasticism, partly due to the fact that Saint Pachomius was very strict in the rules of monasticism, but also because it had been one of Saint Pachomius' disciples who established monasticism in Ethiopia.

Visiting a Doctor in Embaba in el-Gezeera

Father Abd el-Mesih el-Habashi fell sick one day, so much so that when he coughed, worms would come out of his stomach. The Arab Bedouins roaming the desert found him and took him with them to a doctor in Embaba, where he received the pitying looks of all the doctors due to his very bad shape and health. When the doctor set him down on a table and went to get a glucose IV injection, Father Abd el-Mesih quickly and quietly escaped in the doctor's absence. When the doctor came back and noticed the empty bed, they searched everywhere for him and could not find him. After a long and arduous search, the Bedouins finally gave up and went back to the monastery to ask if he had been there. Nobody knew where he was, so they went to his cave and found him there, completely healed and healthy. When they asked him how he had been cured, he would not answer.

Visiting a Village in Wadi el-Natroun

The strangest incident of Father Abd el-Mesih leaving his cave is told by Very Rev Father Mansour el-Baramousy:

"One day Father Abd el-Mesih left his cell and started walking directly towards the monastery of Wadi el-Natroun. He did not know any laypeople from Wadi el-Natroun. He walked very intuitively through the village, stopped at one of the houses, and knocked on the door. A man called Abu Ghayora answered the door. Then Father Abd el-Mesih confronted him with his half-Arabic accent and told him, "Don't divorce your wife...there is a child..." and then just walked away. The man was bewildered at such a strange occurrence, but this man had in fact put in his heart to divorce his wife because she was barren and could not bear him any children, but he had not yet revealed what was in his heart. Instead of divorcing his wife, he decided to put off the decision for a while.

The next year, Father Abd el-Mesih went back the same way to the same person and knocked on his door, and a different person opened it. Father Abd el-Mesih said, "There is a baby today," and it was true: the mother had given birth to a son. The man sensed Father Abd el-Mesih's presence, so he went out and greeted him warmly. Since then, Mr Abu Ghayora devoted his resources to helping Father Abd el-Mesih in whatever way possible. He offered to drive him around wherever he wanted to go, until the day that Father Abd el-Mesih left to go to Jerusalem.

Visiting Pope Kyrollos

Father Abd el-Mesih el-Habashi desired solitude, so he went to Pope Kyrollos in August 1967 and pleaded with him to prohibit visitors to his cell.

His Second Visit to Saint Anthony's Monastery

Mr George Tesphay, in the Ethiopian Embassy, says that when Father Abd el-Mesih el-Habashi went to Cairo, preparing to go to Jerusalem, he asked to visit Saint Anthony's Monastery one last time. Someone from the Patriarchate came to the Embassy to obtain permission – because it was a delicate time of war – but he was refused permission to travel to Saint Anthony's Monastery. Father Abd el-Mesih then said, "If they refuse to permit me from visiting him, he (St. Anthony) will send me himself".

Indeed, the next morning, the abbot of the Monastery of Saint Anthony came to the Papal residence, and while he was there, he found out about Father Abd el-Mesih's request to visit his monastery, so he took him along with him to the monastery. Once again, Father Abd el-Mesih escaped from the monastery and it took people a long time to find him by car! When they finally found him, they took him back to the Papal residence and had to lock him up, presumably because he wanted to continue walking from Saint Anthony's Monastery to Jerusalem.

Visiting the convent in Masr el-Kadeema

Very Rev Father Anastasy el-Samuely recalls the time when Father Abd el-Mesih el-Habashi was in the Papal residency, and he requested to visit some convents, so he offered to take him to a convent, and he immediately accepted. Very Rev Father Anastasy called the convent and asked the abbess to prepare the other nuns to take Father Abd el-Mesih's blessing. Indeed, Father Abd el-Mesih went to the convent, and during his visit, he wanted to say how people broke the commandments even though they knew them, so, in his very broken Arabic, he said, "You know them, and you mix them up!"

Travelling to Jerusalem and His Final Days

All the Ethiopian monks who came to Egypt had the same goal: to finish their struggle in Egypt – the birthplace of monasticism, which had been blessed by the presence of the Holy Family – and then travel to Jerusalem and finish their final days there.

Everybody who visited or met Father Abd el-Mesih

el-Habashi (the Ethiopian) in his final years in Egypt, especially in the early 1960s, found him engulfed with that thought; and as if it were good news, he would tell his visitors, "I am going to Jerusalem." He chose 1972 to leave for Jerusalem, but he told no one of the reason. However, he was very happy and mentally prepared to leave at that time, and he would clearly show his enthusiasm to all his visitors, whether monks, priests or laypeople.

A few months after Pope Shenouda the Third was enthroned as Pope, Father Abd el-Mesih called the man from Wadi el-Natroun who used to help him to come and drive him to the Papal residence in Cairo. When he arrived there, he gave away whatever he owned – such as an axe for cutting wood, a spoon and a scarf – to some fathers, and took his three books with him – the Agpia, the book of the Psalms, and the book about Saint Isaac the Syrian – and went to Cairo.

In Cairo, he met the new Pope and greeted him warmly, and talked to him about travelling to Jerusalem. He even rushed him to allow him to travel. However, Pope Shenouda settled him down and told him to wait until an appropriate time came, as there was a war on between Egypt and Israel at that time.

The Room at the Papal Residence

Due to being delayed, Father Abd el-Mesih el-Habashi took up the Pope's offer of a room to stay in until the paperwork for his journey to Jerusalem was finalised. This room was near the entrance of the College of Coptic Studies, beside the main switchboard. Father Abd el-Mesih asked that his room be fully cleared out, even for the bed to be removed. He asked only for a small mat made of palm leaves, and an old blanket to cover him by night. Everybody who visited him in that room agreed that the room was not fit for a human being to live in.

He usually kept bread and oranges in his room; he would sit there for long periods huddled in a corner, praying or reading his books. His door would only open twice a day, once to eat his only meal of the day in the evening, and again for him to go to the bathroom. He notified workers in the building not to let anyone open his door at any other time, nor to let any visitors come into his room.

Very Rev Father Anastasy el-Samuely concurred on the fact that Father Abd el-Mesih's room was not a room suitable for human occupation. However, from time to time, he would meet some of his visitors outside his room, and they would look inside and feel overwhelmed with guilt for how inhospitable his room looked. They would sit with him outside his room, listening to his enlightening interpretation of the Holy Bible, seasoned with the Holy Spirit. If the number of visitors became too great, he would get upset, get up, and quickly go to his room.

Meeting the Ethiopian Bishops

After a few days he met four Ethiopian bishops who were in Cairo at that time, and he revealed to them his intention of going to Jerusalem, so they took him, along with Father Abd Mariam the Ethiopian (who is currently an Ethiopian Bishop), to the Ethiopian Ambassador's house in Cairo. Mr George Tesphay, who worked in the Embassy, also joined them. They talked for a long time, so when Father Abd Mariam tried to end the meeting – due to the many duties of the bishops – by pulling gently at Father Abd el-Mesih's sleeve, Father Abd el-Mesih did not want the meeting to end yet, probably wanting to make sure that the Ambassador would agree to help him go to Jerusalem. At that moment, the Ambassador asked Mr Tesphay to bring the papers needed for Father Abd el-Mesih's trip, and took a photograph and affixed it to the papers and the passport. Before Father Abd el-Mesih left, the Ambassador asked him to pray for him and bless him, so he replied saying, "Do not think that you will be saved just because I blessed you, O naïve man."

When the papers took a long time to come through, he insisted on travelling to Jerusalem on foot. Those in the Papal residence refused, explaining to him that this was not possible, as he must fly there in a plane. He refused with his typical gentleness, saying that he did not want to ride in a tin box (referring to a plane). They tried explaining to him again that going on foot was nearly impossible due to the war between Egypt and Israel, and that soldiers were hiding behind every corner, but he was only surprised by of the war and that people did not have peace!

Living at the House of the Late Ragheb Moftah

Father Abd el-Mesih el-Habashi finally tired of living in his tiny room in the Papal residence, so he asked the Pope if he could move in with Professor Ragheb Moftah. The Pope agreed to this, knowing that Father Abd el-Mesih really loved Professor Moftah.

Professor Moftah said this about Father Abd el-Mesih el-Habashi: "He stayed with me for three months, and he used to pray all night, and sit on the floor to read the Holy Bible. I do not recall seeing him sleep. His only meal took place in the evening, and he would eat some fasting food, even during the Holy

50 days after the Resurrection. If he had any leftovers from one day, he would hide them under the sofa to eat the following day. I had a little Coptic boy who used to work at home, and one day I told him to go quietly and take the food from underneath the couch. The child cried out loudly when Father Abd el-Mesih grabbed him violently and told him, 'Away from me, you devil.'"

Two Months in Abo Keer in Alexandria

In the early days of June 1972, when the chorus of the Institute of Coptic Studies held a meeting to record some hymns, Father Abd el-Mesih was still living with Dr Moftah, so he could not leave him behind and travel with the chorus. However Dr Moftah convinced him that he should go with them. Mr Moftah relates the following about this incident:

"When summer came, I took him to Abo Keer and we stayed there together for two months. We cooked for him, and fed him, until he said, 'I am a king now!'"

Travelling to Jerusalem

At that time, the paperwork for Father Abd el-Mesih el-Habashi's trip to Jerusalem had been finalised, via confirmation from our church in Beirut from amongst the Diocese of Community Services. He could finally travel to Jerusalem, firstly by ship to Lebanon, then to Amman in Jordan – where it would be possible for him to cross the Elemby Bridge to the Holy Land. He agreed to this and travelled with Dr Isayas Ilmeya.

Very Rev Father Boules el-Mahreky – overseer of the Coptic Church in Beirut – says,

"In June of 1973, I received two letters: one from Pope Shenouda and the other from the late Bishop Samuel, Bishop of Community Services, regarding Father Abd el-Mesih. The letters expressed his desire to live out his final days in Jerusalem, after spending about forty years in the Baramous Monastery. They also said that he would be arriving by ship due to his refusal to travel on a plane. His reason for this was that the Lord Christ used ships and boats to travel when He lived on Earth, and not planes!

I went and awaited his arrival at the appointed time, and took him to one of the deacons' houses in the region called el-Rebwa on the way to Mount Telphia. This was due to his strong refusal to take a room in the church, for he viewed that the facilities provided by the church must not be used for sleep. He also refused to sleep over at a family's house; had it not been for the fact that this deacon's house was frequently visited by the Metropolitan and the priest, he would have refused it as well."

We now read what this deacon says about the time Father Abd el-Mesih spent with him. "Bishop Samuel from the Diocese of Community Services called me and informed me of Father Abd el-Mesih's arrival. I was told that he had gone to Pope Shenouda asking for permission to travel to Jerusalem on foot, that this request had been declined, and that he had been forced to take a ship to Lebanon. In our house, he refused to sleep on a bed, and he asked us if we had a chicken pen where he could spend the night. Of course, we did not have any chickens or any pen! He then agreed to sleep on the balcony of the house and would eat fasting food once a day."

Very Rev Father Boules el-Mahreky added the following:

"Father Abd el-Mesih el-Habashi did not carry a passport with him; he only carried a permit of passage from Egypt to Lebanon. At that time, there was a lot of tension between Lebanon and Syria, and we knew at that time that there was absolutely no relationship between Syria and Ethiopia. Syria is the country lying between Lebanon and Jordan, and therefore the country he had to pass through to reach Jordan. Father Abd el-Mesih's nationality was Ethiopian.

From that point, we had a lot of difficulties trying to have a permit to pass from Lebanon to Jordan approved (so that he could enter Jerusalem). However, the Syrian Orthodox Patriarch offered us a helping hand until we received the approval on the permit."

We now return to Mr Banoub Shehata who continues the story saying:

"After a few days, we took him by car to Damascus to spend the night in the Syrian Diocese. Once again, he slept on the floor. We then accompanied him to the border with Jordan, to continue his trip to Amman. Over there, we discovered that the visa permit he held to stay in Lebanon had already expired. Under normal circumstances, he would have had to return from the border to the national security office in Beirut to renew it, however the Lord granted him favour in the eyes of the soldiers at the border, and they extended his visa (which is very unusual). He is a man of God, and God did not forsake him.

Before they let us through the border, the soldiers had to search us very thoroughly. After they searched the car, they wanted to search Father Abd el-Mesih, but he slapped the hand of one of the guards. Since I know the Ethiopian language (on account of having lived there for some decades), I explained to him that if he did not allow the man to search him, he would not be allowed to continue to travel to Jerusalem. He finally agreed, and the guard started searching him. Father Abd el-Mesih had his three books wrapped up in a linen cloth, hidden under his garment. When the guard found them, he was afraid and embarrassed, and asked me to ask Father to forgive him and pray for him.

When we arrived in Amman, we had already called Metropolitan Basilius of Jerusalem. When he arrived, Father Abd el-Mesih was sitting on the floor, but he did not get up to greet him. Instead, he asked him to sit next to him on the ground, so he did as he was told. Father Abd el-Mesih started rebuking him for wearing such fancy clothes, saying, "Are you not a monk?" So he answered, "Yes." So Father Abd el-Mesih asked him, "Then why do you wear such fancy clothes?" and the Metropolitan sat there silently next to him.

Prophecy of the War in Lebanon

Very Rev Father Boules el-Mahreky said that Father Abd el-Mesih el-Habashi made an accurate prophecy about the destruction of Lebanon.He adds,

"He spent a month with us in Lebanon, during which he asked us many times to let him go to Jerusalem on foot. But he listened to my advice, saying, "If the Pope of Egypt kept me with him for a whole year, then you have every right to keep me with you a few more days." He highly respected the advice of priests and bishops."

In Jerusalem

Details of his life and evidence of his existence disappeared from this period onward. We never heard of him again. Some monks who lived in Jerusalem revealed to us that he never came to Jerusalem and that they have no idea where he went. Dr Isaias Ilmia also confirmed these same sayings to the nephew of Father Abd el-Mesih in Ethiopia.

So where did he spend his final days?

According to our speculations, after a long time of searching, we assume that he spent his final days in one of the Syrian Orthodox monasteries or churches that received him. He presumably knew them from Damascus (as was mentioned previously) and he passed away there.

Many laypeople and priests believe that Father Abd el-Mesih died in Jerusalem. However, Dr Ragheb Moftah – who was the closest person to Father Abd el-Mesih – said that he died five years after leaving Egypt. This means that he died in late 1977 or early 1978.

A Vision Concerning His Body

I met one of the Ethiopian monks, who told me that he had had a vision in which he saw the body of Father Abd el-Mesih in a certain place. This had happened ten years before I met him. He asked that we not mention the details of the vision until we were sure we had found the body in that place.

We ask the Lord to guide us to the place of this holy man's body, which would bring us consolation and many blessings for the church.

SIX

ENCOUNTERS

WHEN FATHER ABD EL-MESIH was due to arrive in Lebanon, the deacon of the Coptic Church in Beirut came out with the priest acting in the position of the pope to meet Father Abd el-Mesih el-Habashi at the harbour. When the ship arrived, people started disembarking, and the deacon and the priest started looking among their faces for Father Abd el-Mesih, when suddenly the priest felt someone prostrating himself at his feet. He looked down and found Father Abd el-Mesih, whom he pulled up and did likewise.

This priest says the following about the saint:

"Father Abd el-Mesih el-Habashi the Ethiopian was of average height, dark skinned and quite noticeably skinny. His body was like dry wood, giving the impression that he did not weigh much. He wore a dark tunic on the skin, and on his head he wore a turban made of cotton. He covered himself with an old blanket, covering his head and part of his shoulders. He hung a basket full of books by a stick on his shoulder. He also used to carry books around inside his garments.

Father Abd el-Mesih had a different look to the rest of the residents of the country. This made people stop and stare at this strangely dressed person. His look caused the national guard to stop him, take him aside and physically search him, in order to try to identify him.

In the inspection room, the deputy chief found that Father Abd el-Mesih kept a book inside his garments, around his chest, so he took it and started looking through it. It was written in an Ethiopian language, and the pages and corners of the books were worn away. He took it and threw it on the floor.

Seeing this man throwing the Holy Bible on the floor, Father Abd el-Mesih el-Habashi could not hold himself back; he collected all his energy and gave the man a mighty slap that caused him to scream out in agony.

The monk accompanying Father Abd el-Mesih was immediately called in to face the deputy chief because of this incident. The intention was to charge him for assaulting a high ranking officer while he was on duty. Anyone would expect harsh outcomes from this incident, as the national guard are free to shoot anyone, or to imprison them without clear cause.

Throughout this tense situation, silence reigned in the room. Before the monk accompanying him could say a word of apology for Father Abd el-Mesih's slap, the deputy chief gave verbal instructions for a clear passage to Jordan for Father Abd el-Mesih and the monk without further delay. So Father Abd el-Mesih passed through a very tough situation which could have ended his life, as well as the life of the monk accompanying him. The monk accompanying him emerged shocked, repeating David the prophet's Psalm: "If it had not been the LORD who was on our side, when men rose up against us, then they would have swallowed us alive." (Psalm 124: 3-4)

He does not drink milk

In the Holy 50 days following the Resurrection, some fathers from the Surian Monastery carried some dried food and a bottle of milk for Father Abd el-Mesih el-Habashi to eat in his cave. He accepted everything except the milk saying, "No... Abd el-Mesih el-Habashi...does not drink milk."

An Offering of Love

One day, Father Abd el-Mesih el-Habashi wanted to offer a fellow monk an offering of love, so he wanted to cook for him. He took a dirty old tin can, filled it with water, and put it on the fire. He added some dried weeds, dried molokheya and tahina. To him, this was a delicious meal and more special than usual to offer to another monk. In Father Tadrous Yacoub's contemplation, Father Abd el-Mesih el-Habashi's actions were not out of asceticism, but the mere fact that the spirit dwelled within him to the extent that his body did not differentiate between good and bad food. What we consider intolerable food could be wonderful and delicious to him.

Drinks Offered to Visitors

Another time, Father Tadrous Yacoub witnessed an incident when a monk made a cup of tea to Father Abd el-Mesih. Father Abd el-Mesih accepted it, added more water and some salt, thinking in himself that he had taken a token of love from that monk.

Which One is Longer?

A conversation ran between a person from the church in Lebanon and Father Abd el-Mesih, during his presence in Beirut.

This person asked him saying, "When you were sitting in your cave with no door, did it ever happen that a wolf came to you?"

"Yes."

"Did a snake ever come to you in the cave?"

"Yes...a big snake...big."

"Did it come face to face with you?"

"Yes, it said, 'ssssssssssss' (the sound a snake makes before it attacks)"

"Did you see its tongue?"

"Yes, I saw it."

Therefore, this person asked him saying, "So which one is longer, a snake's tongue or a man's tongue?"

At this point, Father Abd el-Mesih's eyes shone brightly, and a smile crept to his lips as he said, "No...a man's tongue is longer..."

He meant that the tongue is a dangerous little muscle, as Saint James describes in his book, "Even so the tongue is a little member and boasts great things. See how great a forest a little fire kindles! And the tongue is a fire, a world of iniquity." (James 3: 5-6)

....

TESTAMENT TO THE GREAT ETHIOPIAN

The Words of Father Tadros Malaty

Father Abd el-Mesih el-Habashi, an ascetic monk, lived near the Baramous Monastery for over forty years. He lived the life of the Gospel in the spirit of humility and honesty, in strength and truth. He befriended the beasts of the desert, and fought against nature. He lifted the hearts of many to heaven, and in truth, he lived the life of angels on earth.

The Testimony[4] of Dr. Otto Meinardus[5] (1925-2005)

Today, 4.5 km west of Dair el-Baramus is one of the few
inhabited caves in the ancient Desert of Scetis. Abuna
Abd el-Mesih el-Habashi has lived there since about
1935. Of the three caves, two are used by him. Some
of the equipment of Abuna Abd el-Mesih is without
doubt Second World War material. This solitary goes
to the Dair el-Baramus weekly to obtain water, which
he carries in an old gasoline tin on his head, as well as
some bread. A number of years ago he would carry the
tin full of water. Today, however, due to his age, he can
carry it only half-filled. Abuna Abd el-Mesih is a great
story-teller. During the Second World War, at the time
of Field marshal Rommel's advance in North Africa,
one night the British saw a small fire in the desert
around Dair el-Baramus, and believing it to be that
of a German spy, they began to shoot, almost killing
Abuna Abd el-Mesih. Later on, the British apologized
to Abuna Abd el-Mesih, using the good offices of the
monks of Dair al-Baramus

Though peculiar in many ways, Abuna Abd al-
Mesih was, and still is, a real inspiration to several
Egyptian monks who cherish him greatly. Thus Abuna
Matta al-Maskin (now at Dair Anba Samwil) wanted
to live with him. The Ethiopian, however, in true
Antonian manner,[6] refused to allow Abuna Matta to
come close to him. Only after five days of continuous
persistence and by leading an exemplary eremitical
life, did the Ethiopian receive Abuna Matta who then
stayed with him for several months. Another hermit
influenced by the example of Abuna Abd el-Mesih is
Abuna Antonius el-Surianl, who also lived for a time in
one of the caves near those of the Ethiopian solitary.

I have visited Abuna Abd el-Mesih at two different

occasions and was impressed by his utter indifference to the world. It was difficult for the solitary to understand that a German could be in Egypt, and that, furthermore, a German could also be a Christian. "A German is not, no, never a Christian, for Germans don't believe in God." His strong anti-German reaction is due undoubtedly to his war experience, where he was taken by the British for a German spy.

The food which we brought along, the hermit refused, expressing his disgust by informing us that he would give it to the Bedouins. "God gives me my daily bread, you don't have to come and feed me." While trying to convince him that he should eat a little more to keep, healthy, he merely answered: "When I am sick I enjoy the blessings of God even more, what else can I want than the blessings of God." When Abuna Antonius suggested a wooden door for his cell he merely retorted : "A wolf doesn't need a door, does he?" He continued his discourse by saying: "All the monks, for that matter especially those at Dair el-Baramus and, Dair el-Surian are making war against me, telling me to eat and eat. "They should know better that when you eat oil and fish (sardines), the devil will visit you at night, and you are at the mercy of the devil." In 1958, Abuna Abd el-Mesih left his cave for the first time to be taken to a physician in Alexandria. The doctor admonished him to eat, but the food which he received from him he merely passed on to the driver of the car. "My doctor is Jesus Christ, my food is Jesus Christ, my fuel is Jesus Christ."

The personality of Abuna Abd el-Mesih reveals many characteristics of Oriental psychology, and it is not easy for the Western Christian to understand the dynamics of this solitary monk. That these however, are real, is evident from the influence he has had on, at

least: three people who already have made a distinct
contribution to the Christian Church in Egypt: Abuna
Matta el-Maskin, Abuna Antonius el-Suriani and
Abuna Mina el-Muttawahad el-Baramusi or Anba
Kyrillos VI, the 116th Patriarch.

The Testimony[7] of Dr. John Watson[8]

Stories concerning the Ethiopian's relations with wild
animals are legion. What valour of faith was in Abuna
Abd el-Mesih and what poverty of spirit in those who
simply watched him with his own wild style of life.
Evidence is as one would expect at this time, rather
thin. But in his desert cave Abouna Abd el-Mesih el-
Habashi is said to have spoken of lizards, snakes and
scorpions as "his friends".

Even a very large and dangerous snake is said
to have lived with el-Habashi for some years, the
monstrous snake would come and sit next to him
or even lie down on his lap. Jackals are said to have
slept at the cave entrance. Abuna Abd el-Mesih is
reported to have lived with a wolf in 1964: the wolf in
the cave used to sit with him and he patted it on the
back, allowing the tawny-grey mammal, which had
a formidable reputation for flesh eating, to leave the
cave if visitors came to see the Ethiopian mystic.

Once a gigantic snake came to Abuna Abd el-Mesih
and blew something into his face, but the desert monk
was unafraid. He would even walk out into the desert
carrying a scorpion in his hand. He showed no signs
of fear when handling scorpions, disregarding the
lobster-like pincers and jointed tail that could easily
inflict poison upon anyone touching such a dangerous
arachnid. (1 Kings 12:11). Abuna Abd el-Mesih was
deeply offended when visiting monks killed scorpions

in his cave. He described all life forms in the natural world as his "family".

When once challenged to fit a wooden door to the mouth of his cave for reasons of personal security, Abuna Abd el-Mesih replied, "A jackal does not need a door, does he?" He also liked to quote (Job 5:17). "For you will be in league with the stones of the field; and the beasts of the field will be at peace with you."

Perhaps all stories of love between humans and beasts in any century, from the fourth century and even to our own, are parables of mutual love:

"With Christ every brute beast is wise and every savage creature gentle" (Sulpicius Severus 350-420 Century was a French monk who visited the Copts in Egypt at the end of the fourth century).

Eight

....

CONCLUDING REMARKS

This was the life of Fr Abd el Mesih el-Habashi with all its strict asceticism and miraculous acts. We presented his life, his thought and his sayings, but the question remains, are we asked to apply these strict ascetic practices in our life in order to be good Christians?

The answer is "certainly not" this was his life, it only suited him. It was the result of his personal relationship with Christ, and His commandments, as well as the wealth of monastic figures that he took as example. This was his way of understanding of virtue, and his interpretation of the monastic solitude.

What we can learn from his life though is his asceticism in food and clothing and possession only in moderation and to our spiritual level. How he felt that he was a part of the Church which is the body of Christ and how he interacted with her and was always praying for her. We could also learn from him, his strictness with himself and how he persisted on his values and on achieving his goals.

To glory... and to the crown of life that does not parish our dear father. Depart and rest in the place where there is no sadness, sickness, or hardship and listen to the voice full of joy saying "go into you fatherly embrace" (Matt 25:21).

Remember us in your prayers so we may complete our struggle in peace.

Notes:

1. Bananas grow abundantly in Ethiopia, so these were picked before they ripened, dried and then boiled.
2. The Abbot was Rev Father Basillius the elder, who was known for his strict and tough nature.
3. This cave was previously occupied by a monk named Sarabamoun and before him was Fr Abd el Mesih Saleeb el Masoudi.
4. This passage was taken from, Otto F.A. Meinardus. *"Monks and Monasteries of the Egyptian Deserts."* AUC, Cairo, 1989.
5. Dr. Otto Meinardus was born in 1925 in Hamburg, Germany, and studied theology and sociology in Hamburg, London, St Louis, Chicago, and Boston. From 1956-1968 he was a professor at the American University Cairo. Dr Meinardus is a prolific writer, he wrote numerous books and articles about the Coptic Orthodox Church. He is generally recognised as one of the most authoritative contemporary historian of the Coptic church.
6. St. Antony at first refused to let Paul the Simple live with him. Only after several days of fasting was he admitted by the great Hermit.
7. This passage was taken from, Coptic Church Review, *Volume 27, Number 2, 34-57*
8. Since 1981 Dr Watson has been heavily involved in studying the Coptic, church, saints and culture. He had prolonged visits to Egypt during which he was able to live among the monks of Egypt. He wrote many articles about contemporary Coptic figures, one of which is our saint, Fr abd el-Mesih el-Habashi.

www.ingramcontent.com/pod-product-compliance
Lightning Source LLC
Chambersburg PA
CBHW060401090426
42734CB00011B/2222